Letters from the Heart

John Main

LETTERS
from the HEART

*Christian Monasticism
and the Renewal of Community*

CROSSROAD · NEW YORK

ACKNOWLEDGMENTS

All biblical quotations are from *The New English Bible;*
Oxford University Press, 1961
© The Delegates of the Oxford University Press
and the Syndics of the Cambridge University Press 1961.

1991

The Crossroad Publishing Company
370 Lexington Avenue, New York, NY 10017

Printed in the United States of America

Library of Congress Catalog Card Number: 81-70883
ISBN: 0-8245-0444-5

Contents

Introduction   7

Letter One   38

Letter Two   42

Letter Three   50

Letter Four   60

Letter Five   68

Letter Six   77

Letter Seven   86

Letter Eight   97

Letter Nine   105

Letter Ten   111

Letter Eleven   121

Letter Twelve   127

Introduction

In 1974 I returned to my own monastery in London, England, after serving for five years as headmaster of the school at St. Anselm's Abbey in Washington, D.C. Each of these years as I spoke to the graduating class I wondered how well we Western monks had prepared these young men for their lives in the world. Would they know life in the dimension of Spirit, as a mystery rooted in the joy of being? Or would their contact with life be restricted to the sense of a struggle for success to which the fading memory of their monastic schooling would become increasingly irrelevant?

All through these years in the most success-oriented of all cultures I had been thinking of a more really spiritual contribution that Western monasticism could make to our society. How could we open our own heritage of meditation and spiritual discipline to our contemporaries and share it with them in the confidence that it was both real and present? And now, with my return to London, the opportunity to try to do this arose. With the support of the Abbot and the community at Ealing Abbey, we started a spiritual center in a large house on the edge of the property alongside the monastery. Our aim was simple and moderate—we were not running courses on spirituality or going for numbers and the appearance of busyness. But our aim, too, was quite clear and precise. We would invite men to come and live our life with us there for a limited period of time in the hope that during their stay we would be able to teach them to meditate. The tradition out of which we would teach was that of Western monasticism from its beginning: the teaching of John Cassian, invoked as a spiritual guide in the Rule, and St. Benedict's "teacher of prayer." And in imitation of both of these founders of the Benedictine tradition, we were clear that the essential way to teach others how to pray is to pray with them.

We began with a small group of young laymen who heard what we were starting and came to us asking if they could learn to meditate with us. As so often happens with enterprises that begin in this way, the development of our initial idea revealed an inner logic we had not understood at first, and following it led us into a wholly unpredicted perspective full of opportunity both for a radical monastic self-renewal and for reinvesting the monastic life with contemporary relevance.

One of the first things that the presence of seriously spiritual laymen in our monastery made us consider was the present relevance and utility of our own monastic life and practice. Like many monasteries we were deeply involved, by our own history, in external works — a school and parish. These, despite our being somewhat overstretched, were flourishing and enriched by much generosity in time and energy from the monks. But as a result, the Divine Office had come to occupy the central place in the community's life of monastic prayer. The relationship between work and the Office, often a tense relationship when time is short, can then become the essential "spiritual" relationship in a monk's life. In the absense of a stimulus for radical self-evaluation, the ongoing conversion of life St. Benedict enjoins on his disciples, it is easy for a disastrous imbalance in the monastic balance between prayer, work, and study to creep in and establish itself unawares and then be transmitted from one monastic generation to another.

The laymen meditating in the center we had started were such a stimulus for self-knowledge. It soon became evident that the main emphasis in the spiritual development they knew was not found primarily in the recitation of the Divine Office but in the practice of silence, ever more interiorized in meditation. Indeed, it seemed to them that the Office, which they attended with perfect fidelity, could only be understood at all if it was approached from silence and led to silence. Nor was this silence institutional, the result of rules. It was the silence they were discovering as a living presence in their own hearts, which was with them at all times and places, in all activities, in community or solitude. It was the expanding inner atmosphere in which they saw reality in depth and in the infinite perspective that makes wonder an essential part of our lives. It was the silence they were beginning to discover, with amazement, as the worship of God.

Our own practice, too, for those meditating with the community of laymen, soon became one of a silence that was more all-embracing than the silence in the monastery itself. We became more aware not only of the power of this silence, which was both an inner reality and the medium of being with others, but also of its fragility. The satellite community, for example, had no television or radios in its house, none of the institutionalized distractions that can so disastrously become part of modern life. The whole atmosphere and the conventions by which the house operated were specifically directed toward prayer. In the early days we prepared for meditation by listening to some music together, but soon everyone came to understand that the best preparation for the silence of meditation and the most appropriate response to the immediate period after it is silence itself.

The life of this small community grew and deepened quietly and unobtrusively. It was no part of its meaning to proselytize for either itself or its teaching, but it was of its very essence to be open to the mystery of its own being, and this it was soon called upon to share. Word of what we were doing began to spread and this led to another unexpected development: the arrival of many lay men and women of all ages and conditions of life and of many religions who came to ask if they too could share in the instruction on meditation we were giving and join us for our actual periods of meditation.

This was not what we had intended to happen nor was it altogether clear at first that it was what we should do. The problems of space and timetabling were minor, but the danger of a shift of emphasis in the new community from residential to transient groups seemed to threaten the purity of the evolving monastic spirit. A number of factors led us to see that this danger was illusory and a product of fear. There was, above all, the essential principle of our life based on meditation, which was the principle of openness to reality—a reality not seen in terms of our own limitations but known as a mystery greater than ourselves and containing us. We could not, then, lay down conditions for our openness. This would be treating the monastic pilgrimage like a package tour selected for its capacity to entertain. If men and women who could not abandon their responsibilties to family or work to come and live with us for six months nevertheless seriously wanted to learn to pray and follow the inner journey as generously as their conditions of life permitted, then it fell to us to give whatever we had received in order to help and strengthen their resolve. The seriousness and perseverance of the people who had sought us out and returned regularly to ask us when we would be starting groups for nonresidents was the deciding factor. We let our initial resistance drop and immediately felt ourselves carried by the stream.

The speed of the current surprised us all. In a short time there were nine separate groups coming to the house weekly. They ranged in size from five to thirty people and in age from teenagers to octogenarians. For each group and at each meeting we had essentially the same message. The practical instruction on how to meditate was easily given at the first meeting, though, of course, in view of its unfamiliarity it needed to be repeated fairly frequently in the early stages—it is so difficult for us to believe that anything so simple could be so absolute. Holding to its simplicity and not giving way to the temptation to complicate for the sake of cleverness or sophistication—this was the main practical reason why people returned each week. We urged them all to meditate every day of the week between their visits to us and to meditate twice a day, once in the morning and once in the evening. We repeated this message week after week—to be simple, to be faithful. As the groups deepened their commitment we gradually developed, in our opening talks, a theology of meditation based on the "secret" of St. Paul's letters, the indwelling Spirit of God in the human heart, "the secret of Christ in you." But even this developing theology, wonderful as it was to see and feel evolve as the groups matured, was not the reason for our meeting. As any one of the groups would say, they came above all to meditate together. The half hour of silence was of far greater power and enduring significance than anything said before in the opening talk or anything discussed together afterward. Very often, with the more experienced groups, there would be no questions or points raised, and with a wonderful mutual confidence, people would leave in silence.

From this early development of our center it seemed to us that we had stumbled upon—or been led to—two elements in our situation that could perhaps point the way forward to a monasticism of the future. The first of these was the incredible richness of our own Christian monastic tradition of meditation lying latent before us and effectively closed to us until we took the step into the experience that would open its treasures to us. *Experientia magistra*, a phrase from Cassian's *Conferences*, kept recurring in my mind—experience is the teacher. Perhaps only the incredible confidence of the New Testament itself would persuade those trained to distrust "experience" as another form of "singularity" that the experience of prayer was our experience of the person of Christ. It was an experience in which the one experiencing experiences with the full consciousness of the one who is experienced: a union of love that the familiar pages of the New Testament put before us in words we had somehow failed to understand on the level at which they demanded to be heard. What else did it mean to say that "we possess the mind of Christ"?

The richness of the monastic tradition of meditation grew directly out of the richness of the gospels, and the vital connection, as we said to the groups, was poverty. It is the poor in spirit who find that the kingdom is not a place but an experience of the person who is one with Love. Meditation, central to the whole monastic tradition, is the way to become poor in spirit. The message was addressed and still addresses itself universally, but the monk is there, separated from men but in harmony with all, to prove that it is both believable and possible, and that the practicality of the journey to the kingdom is daily perseverance in the experience of deepening poverty. The early days of beginning to meditate can be ones of great enthusiasm as one opens up a world of spiritual richness he or she had not dreamed existed—the "first fervor of conversion," as St. Benedict called it. But the hinge upon which we swing into the really transcendent experience is the fidelity and regularity of commitment that does not concern itself with "good" meditations or "bad" meditations. There is only one meditation—the one where we are faithful to the deepening of our poverty.

We already had begun to learn for ourselves that the commitment to a daily practice of meditation introduced us to a developing theology and one that grew in our own hearts. We learned what Evagrius meant by saying, "A theologian is one who prays and one who prays is a theologian." As we talked to the groups out of this knowledge, it sometimes seemed strange that *they* did not find it stranger. What we were teaching was what Cassian had taught at the beginning and the tradition had passed on from one generation to another. But the teaching was unfamiliar even to many monks and scholars of the texts. Yet here were growing numbers of lay people, with busy lives and heavy responsibilities, building in a transcendent commitment to poverty of spirit, of mind, and of heart into their daily lives; and knowing from their own faith what it meant to say that their concern was not "to experience the experience" but the experience-in-itself. The discipline of the silence we shared each week together and each day in our own places led us into realms of knowledge that simply cannot be explored in a self-conscious or merely speculative way. And this is surely one of the great gifts that monasticism has to offer world and church—the experiential knowledge born of faith that underpins the whole self-communication of Christ in his Body. It was with a sense of wonder that was not of the moment, not just a thrill, but a wonder that pervaded their consciousness more thoroughly from week to week that many in the groups began to *see* what before they had just looked at—to see the meaning of the gospel stories, of St. Paul, and of the Eucharist that we now held weekly in the house, meditating after the Communion. People did not suddenly come to these insights. Their way began in faith and they were ready to believe that it would end in faith. But the wonder was there and it was growing. The level at which our experience is real was getting steadily deeper, and as it deepened it brought forth that knowledge we call wisdom.

This was the first of the elements that made us think of the new monasticism that would regain its central spiritual function in the world—the latent richness of its own tradition realized in the experience of prayer. The second element was the other side of an equation that converted self-discovery into other-centeredness. The newly awakened monasticism would be called forth by the spiritual crisis of its own time and place. We were familiar enough with the existence of such a crisis. What we began to see more sharply was that it was not just a crisis of materialism, of a loss of spiritual values. The crisis was more painful to contemplate than that. The crisis was the men and women of deep spiritual seriousness and hunger who were being denied the vital reference points of their growth to maturity and who lacked the personal communication of teaching authority and experience—it was these who really were the crisis. Their crisis was the crisis of our society, which had lost its experience of Spirit. These were the real apostles on whom the building up of the Body depended. They were the catalyst that changed matter into the Body. And if these ordinary people living and working in the world lacked the transforming experience in their own hearts, where would be their power to transform their world in love? They came to us for the most part because they felt they did lack it, though exactly what "it" was they would not all perhaps have been able to say. They knew, often in a very simple faith trained in the old ways, that ritual obedience and personal devotions could not of themselves be the gospel experience. They felt the void but were no longer content to try to fill it in with religious distraction. They knew that the only way to transform the emptiness into plenitude was to enter it in person.

At our center many of them found a context where the faith necessary for this journey could be found. And in our faith-less society perhaps this is a monastery's preeminent service, to be a place where faith is lived, honored, and communicated. It is a place where very ordinary men, not spiritual giants, prove that faith is possible and necessary. Perhaps what I have been saying has underemphasized the ordinariness of the people concerned in our center, but it was an ordinariness touched by sublimity—the sublimity of the knowledge of Christ.

This sublimity, in fact, constituted the creative spirit that everyone involved in what we were doing felt at work. It came from the presence of a wonderful and liberating paradox among us. We were ordinary people becoming aware of the invitation to sublimity that the gospel addresses to us all. Our awareness itself was being born out of a personal discovery of the genuineness of the central paradox of Christ's teaching—that we must lose our life in order to find it. And the unifying focal point of all these facets of the mystery was not an idea, a theology, or an image, but the simple and simplifying practice of meditation.

So, very early on in our work, it became clear that only a monasticism vitalized by a return to its principal task of "seeking God" in prayer would be able to reestablish an authentic relationship with the world. This relationship has to be and can only be a bond of spiritual energy if monasticism is true to itself and monks to their vocation. Our development had suggested more precisely what this relationship might be. The lay people who came were in serious and profound search for a way to enter into the direct and personal experience of God and, if they were Christians, they believed that this meant the way of prayer—a prayer that could no longer be defined as talking to God or thinking about God, but a prayer that could only be described as their awareness of God in Jesus. They came to learn how to enter this experience as our common tradition had taught us. And they came to receive the support and continuing encouragement both of those who had made it the absolute priority of their lives and of those who, like themselves, were following the way as it led through the normal responsibilities and situations of life.

It is true, then, to say that the new relationship of monks to the world will include a teaching function. The people who came to us to learn to meditate were those who possessed the humility, the realistic self-knowledge, to want to learn and to be teachable. But to say we were teachers of prayer needs a serious qualification. We were talking to people whose humilty had brought them to an experiential knowledge of St. Paul's unforgettable remark that "we do not know how to pray." They were, that is to say, ordinary people of some spiritual maturity. As Cassian put it, "You are on the brink of knowledge if you attentively recognize what you should ask about and you are not far from knowledge if you begin to understand how much you do not know" (*Conferences* X:ix). It was not surprising, therefore, that our groups were most affected by the teaching that instruction has a very limited value. Anything that can be said is by its nature preparatory for the silence in which the experience, the teaching, and the teacher are one. Our repeated message was that the only way to the experience is the practice. Nor was it surprising that we had the good fortune to learn for ourselves at the beginning that to teach others how to meditate really means to meditate with them.

None of these insights was instantaneous. They arose and were tested by events as we developed during the first two years of the center. At the end of that period we were faced with another opportunity far more radically demanding and unpredictable than the arrival of people asking to share our tradition. Word of our center was spreading in all directions, partly through personal contact, partly through the first of our publications. By a peculiar series of connections, news of our work reached Montreal through both these means and brought us an invitation from the Archbishop of Montreal to make a foundation there along the lines we were following in London. He and Bishop Leonard Crowley, the Auxiliary Bishop in charge of English Language Affairs, described the kind of monastic spiritual resource center they felt their people needed and placed the proposal before the Ealing community.

The invitation was unanimously turned down. The community naturally felt honored at the invitation and was also responsive to the idea of making a contribution to the universal church. Nevertheless, Ealing felt unable to respond more positively to the Montreal proposal because of its own manpower problem. No one, it was felt, could be spared. But their first refusal, far from deterring Bishop Crowley, seemed to increase his own faith in the idea, and he persistently put his vision of it before us. His determination won through, and at the beginning of 1977 the Abbot of Ealing changed his mind.

The situation had been changed by the lay people of the community coming to our rescue. Four of them had offered to support a foundation by coming with one or two monks to help start. Brother Laurence Freeman, a monk at Ealing in simple vows who had embarked on his theological studies, had volunteered to come, and so the founding members were formed: two monks leaving familiar ground to start what we knew would be a new type of monastery and four lay people leaving jobs and families to help them.

* * *

Starting our monastery in Montreal from scratch, with none of the buildings and few of the resources most monasteries can call upon in need, gave us a unique opportunity to confront the bare essentials of monasticism. In a most unlikely and unexpected way we found ourselves transported from a monastic life in which the means of livelihood and service, the daily structure of work and worship, were all received. They could, of course, be changed or adapted, but underlying any change in the inherited monasticism was the preference for long-established custom.

From custom we were thrown back upon the bedrock of tradition. In Montreal we had only this tradition as a present reality alive in our experience of prayer. We felt as if we were discovering for the first time that "tradition" has life and meaning; that tradition becomes just a historical memory when it is not one with personal experience. To say that the tradition and the experience are one, in the moment of love, seemed to be the most important contemporary message for monasticism. This experience of prayer, which all of us shared, and the formation in the Rule of St. Benedict that the monks knew, were the basic elements in the new community we watched and felt grow, both within us and around us, in the months ahead. For the refinement of our sense of the monastic spirit this was a crucial time, and it led us into a sharper understanding of the Rule as the great monastic document it is — the Rule that with all its gentleness and human tolerance is marked by an uncompromising rigor in leading the monk to seek God as the first responsibility of his life.

Our relationship with the city, the Church, and our new continent in general began from this responsibility and the experience of the tradition that was our mainstay. We had neither school nor parish nor any kind of external apostolate. And so it became clear straightaway that our monastic life and the witness that is an indispensable part of it would only be effective if our experience of the spiritual reality to which we had committed ourselves opened up a line of direct communication with this new and complex type of society. This communication would be the monastic *word*. And its being truly monastic would mean that, complex and changeable as was the society we found ourselves in, our *word* would have to be simple and emanate from a living tradition. An honest and uncompromising contact with the realities of contemporary urban life, far from distorting our life in the monastery, would be an invaluable opportunity to refine and simplify it more effectively and more quickly than is always possible in an inherited cloister. This was so because the world, in a small way, was coming to us, and its mobility, joined creatively with our stability, was to form a new kind of cloister. Our direct communication with the city originated in the *word* they demanded of us as men whose outward form of life was supposed to point to a level of spiritual reality, a spiritual continuum below the world's restlessness. It was a demand made in friendship but also a challenge to prove that what we had come to say had the same contemporary significance as the *word* that Alexandria came out to the desert to beg of the first Christian monks. The *word* was the same; it was not a question of trying to be original. The challenge was to find the medium that would make it glow.

Before leaving England I had made three cassettes on prayer. They were made at different times and in response to needs that arose out of our work at the center in London to teach people how to meditate—a work that is largely taken up with persuading people of the simplicity of meditation. Nearly everyone who came asked what they should read on prayer and very few were content to be told to read nothing on prayer at all—until they had begun to meditate and discovered why. But we recommended a slow and careful reading of Scripture as an essential part of a mature Christian life—the *lectio* of the Rule. And there were a few books (usually not bestsellers) that could be enriching companions of one's pilgrimage for a lifetime—books that included Abhishiktananda's *Saccidananda*. Our own cassettes were made for ongoing use in this way, not to define prayer or reveal the "secret art" but ultimately and increasingly to point away from the individual person to the actual practice of meditation and to perseverance in it.

The first cassette, "Introduction to Christian Meditation," was a practical response to people visiting us in London for brief stays who wanted to take away with them a statement of our essential practice that they could share with their friends or communities, as well as to use themselves, as an aid for their own beginning in meditation. The four talks on the tape brought together, in a condensed way that demanded a certain effort of concentration, the substance of the introductory talks we gave to groups of beginners coming to the center one evening a week. The substance was as simple as the message—why any one of us wants to begin this journey, the tradition of previous Christian generations who have felt the same call and responded to it, and, most important, the method and the absolute demand of the method.

It seemed then to me, and does still, that the spoken word is the essential medium for the communication of the gospel. The experience of the gospel is the fullest personal experience of communion, and it communicates itself between persons alive to themselves and to each other as persons. One can, of course, pour one's personhood into a book, but it will be only rarely that any reader can both receive this gift and assimilate it into his or her own self-giving. Nor can we ever be sure that print carries the tone of voice that we read in it. These problems of communication are lessened in the spoken word and the demand for concentration, without which there is no communication in any medium, is humanized. And, above all, the communication of the gospel in the spoken word makes it possible to present the absolute call of Christ as something not idealistic but eminently practical. Not "*a man* must lose his life," but "*you* must lose *your* life."

Listening to a tape, in the absence of the speaker, at least maintains the discipline of listening. As I said at the beginning of the first talk, if you can listen to this tape carefully you are taking your first step in learning to meditate, because to meditate is to listen to the word. In the early days of our literate culture, the link between the book and the spoken word was not broken — St. Benedict warns his monks not to read too loudly while at their private *lectio*; and St. Augustine was reading aloud from his Bible when his great awakening occurred. Today our books are too private experiences that rarely communicate themselves to others. We tend to be turned upon ourselves, our own reactions, and our own intelligence when we read in the way most of us have been trained. Obviously, there have also been advantages in the private reading of books — systems of thought that it would be next to impossible to communicate orally can be lucidly rendered in silent print. But, when we are talking of prayer or of the essential *personal* dimension of the gospel experience, we are not dealing with a system of thought but with a *word*, unified and centered in a person. Our teaching of meditation was an attempt to communicate this word as the *logos*, which is the universe in which all thought or imagination or language are secondary reflections of the primary experience of the mystery of God in his transcendence of our limited forms of knowledge. To know God we have to abandon our own habits of knowledge and enter into his own self-knowledge; and this is the work of silence.

The spoken word seemed able to lead people to this silence more effectively. If, in reading this book, you feel drawn to explore the way of meditation as a possibility for yourself, I would strongly advise you to listen to the talks on the original cassettes. Both the book and the tapes are poor substitutes for a fully personal communication, the teacher and the community that constitute the heart of the monastic tradition. But it is in the intrinsic nature of the journey to find these when the *logos–logic* of your growth demands it. All we have to do is to begin.

The first cassette had the preeminently practical aim of encouraging people to begin and to persevere. The second tape, made about a year later, addressed itself to those who had begun and were persevering. As the theology of meditation grew out of our experience within the community and in contact with the groups, it seemed natural to communicate this also. It was not meant to be an "abstract" theology designed as a primarily intellectual stimulus. Nor was it anti-intellectual. The complaint that some people made about meditation—that it was "nonincarnational" because it rejected the intellectual part of man—could only be made before the experience of meditation had been entered into: the experience of the integration of mind and heart in a silence beyond the limitations of the self-reflective consciousness. The experience of this integration pervades the whole mystery of the meditator's life. When people would ask how they could tell if they were making progress in meditation, since they were not supposed to analyze or assess their actual periods of meditation, the answer would usually be self-evident. A greater rootedness in self, a deeper emotional stability, a greater capacity to center in others and away from self were the signs of spiritual growth. To the Christian this could be expressed more simply as becoming more loving and more aware of love as the essential energy of life. For most people these were the signs of the journey beyond itself. But for many, too, there was the sense of a greater intellectual simplicity and clarity. What had before seemed to them expressible only in complex and self-qualifying terminology now began to be perceived in its self-evidencing immediacy—its being not an idea but a reality. The power of knowing what had before only been speculated upon bestowed new gifts of expression and a sharper way of communicating. Very often the starting point of a new intellectual clarity would be a fresh experience of the *word* communicated in the New Testament or a new "reading" of one's own immediate situation or vocation. None of these moments or ways of growth, however, were either forced or analyzed. They manifested themselves only in the progressive loss of self-consciousness, the loss of our most precious possession. But what was gained in this loss was beyond our expectation or our power to explain. The liberation of heart and the expansion of mind led more deeply into that integration of consciousness in which our most eloquent and communicable response is simply wonder.

"The Christian Experience," our second tape, was an attempt to communicate something of the wonder we had felt in entering the Trinitarian dimension of prayer. Our own evidently limited experience was a way of lighting up the far greater understanding made available to us, in the common mind all Christians share, through the tradition both of scripture and the great teachers of the Church. We moved from experience to tradition, back to experience, always grounding what we grew in understanding of by the rhythm of our regular return to meditation and the silence "fitting for disciples." This led us to a deeper sense of what Montreal would soon teach us more directly: the congruity of tradition and experience in the moment of prayer, which is the moment of our openness to the person of love. It taught us too what is for me the deepest personal conviction of monastic life and its witness: the conviction that to know God we have first to know ourselves and that we can only fully know ourselves in the moment of prayer. This is the moment of the evaporation of all multiplicity and division, the transcendence of the idea of consecutive states of knowledge (as if we knew ourselves and *then* knew God), and the revelation that all knowing is known within the self-knowing of God, which is his Love. The second of our tapes tried to put this forward as the supreme mystery that motivated the absolute simplicity and deepening poverty of our meditation. We left self behind in order to find our own enduring reality, to find ourselves one with the Father.

The final tape of the set of three, "Twelve Talks for Meditators," was written and made in response to the needs of missionaries. The first tape aimed to lead people to begin, the second to deepen their understanding of the context in which they followed the way, and the third to help them to persevere. Some Sisters of the Medical Missionaries of Mary had invited me to take part in their renewal program and I spoke to two groups at their Mother House in Drogheda. In the course of these talks I suggested how careful we had to be of working for a merely religious renewal at the level of structure and image. There would be no effective renewal in the church despite all the energy expended on courses, meetings, and reorganization if there was not a radical renewal in spirit. This radical renewal in spirit, because of its depth and the nature of its own mystery, was not within our active power to bring about. What we had to do, though, was to prepare ourselves for the power that would effect it. Our preparation is our openness, our vulnerability to the power of God dwelling in us; and this is our prayer. Religious renewal comes down to a renewal in prayer.

Talking to these Sisters, I was greatly moved both by their sincerity and their enthusiasm in really wanting this inner renewal. But I was equally struck by the difficulty of what I was proposing to them. Their lives were demanding and unpredictable and often their schedule was overturned just at the moment when it seemed possible to find time and space for regular hours of prayer. They spoke also of the loneliness of the missionary life in many places and of the problems involved in keeping on with prayer when far away from a spiritual director or the other aids and supports of the religious life. There was no question of meditation not being relevant to them, no question of this being a contemplative's form of prayer unsuitable to their active lives. They knew the universality of the call of the gospel and recognized the way meditation responded to this call. It was a question of human strength and the practicalities of living.

It was with them and their difficulties in mind that I wrote the "Twelve Talks" as short "boosters" designed to encourage and lead the meditators who are on their own to be faithful to their twice-daily times of prayer. In this sense they are as useful to family groups or city workers as to missionaries, and they try to locate meditation in the common human predicament of accepting and growing in the actual situation life has formed for us. Because this situation is for so many today one of loneliness or isolation, the talks stress the vital connection of living prayer with living community. For those praying alone it is important to know that even in the absence of a physically visible community the very commitment they make to pray leads them into a spiritual community that can in subtler ways give the human strength and encouragement we all, saints and sinners, need — the community of those who are faithful and whose faith allows them in moments of grace to recognize each other.

These three tapes, together with a little book of conferences introducing meditation to the beginner, were soon in fairly wide circulation. Because of these and the growing numbers of people visiting the Center in London, several groups of meditators had come together in various places to provide the context of a faithful community to their pilgrimage, and these groups still continue to meet weekly. It was to keep in touch with these groups and many individuals who were on their own in meditation that we began to send out a newsletter from Montreal. It was designed to give more than the minutiae of our development, though the details of our community life were not unrelated to the more solid *doctrina*, or encouragement in the form of teaching, that itself developed out of our lived practice of prayer and concrete experience.

As with our other ventures we soon found that the newsletters were developing into something more than we had expected or intended. Our mailing list grew in North America before long to the size of the European list and people with whom we had had contact only through our publications were now asking to receive a copy. One of the consequences of this was that the newsletter was being read by people who had neither met us nor begun to meditate. Not surprisingly, therefore, we began to receive letters from people who were confused either by the assumptions our *doctrina* took for granted in the reader or by the vocabulary we had developed. What these inquiries also revealed, however, was the far deeper confusion and misunderstanding about prayer in general.

This confusion was often first exposed in a misunderstanding of the word *meditation* itself. We knew, of course, that we were using it in its original, monastic sense of imageless prayer. And we knew that this meaning clashed with the more general meaning meditation had, in Christian circles, of discursive prayer with a great emphasis on the use of imagination. On the other hand, the majority of our contemporaries, especially of the younger generation, understood by meditation exactly what we meant—an understanding they had gained by contact with Eastern religious thought. We continued to use the word *meditation* even to people who understood it differently because the surprise of discovering its traditional meaning could often be, for them, an opportunity to rethink their received ideas on prayer. The tragedy for so many Christians was that these ideas bore so little relationship to the essential, living tradition of their faith.

So many thought of prayer in terms of "types" and "methods," and they had received elaborate systems by which to analyze and categorize prayer-states. The result had inevitably to be an intensification of the very self-consciousness and self-obsession that is the greatest enemy and negation of prayer. Often people would make genuine and generous attempts to enter the mystery of prayer more deeply only to find themselves misled by their own training from manuals of prayer and thrown off course by self-objectification: is this the prayer of quiet, of simple regard, of infused contemplation? These were the more old-fashioned categories, but even the more modern ones encouraged the person trying to pray to remain self-centered and indeed to intensify his or her self-analysis.

It was within this triumph of confusion about the real simplicity of prayer that so many came to hear about meditation through the newsletter or our publications. For many people, what we were saying seemed so opposed to the theory of prayer they had followed as faithfully as they could for a lifetime that they would react with some hostility. For others, their approach was more tolerant—this was a new method of prayer that had to have a place in the received schemes and should be examined on its merits as a "technique." The most frequently heard objection to meditation—one that often came from religious—was that it was "one-sided," concentrating on our spiritual side to such a degree that it rejected our reason and imagination and so could not be truly called incarnational.

The distinction between "spiritual" and "incarnational" approaches to prayer is a feature of the religious climate of our day. It is one that has to be accepted but I have never found that the confusion both of logic and theology that underlies it can be easily solved by much discussion. We all become attached to our own terms and definitions, and if these are themselves confused, the discussion that revolves around them rarely seems to get grounded in reality. Our own approach, therefore, to people who wanted to debate the validity of meditation could sometimes seem arrogant. We said simply what we had to say but only felt discussion worthwhile if it was oriented toward a moment when we would stop discussing and begin to pray together. There were, of course, always genuine questions to answer and terms to explain, but it was usually the case that, if there were not an underlying mutual acceptance of the priority of silence, all the talking led nowhere and became an endless end-in-itself.

The present confusion in many Christian circles about prayer is serious and has to be resolved. But it is only resolvable, in terms of the reality of the practice of prayer, if there is a willingness to let go. And we have to let go of everything. Any discussion about prayer should be a preparation for this act of faith in which we let go of all thinking and defining. It is an irony of our religious mentality that this letting go can itself become an image and a way of thinking. Because of this some people respond excitedly to meditation in the first encounter, thinking that they find in it the way to escape from the diminishing returns of other kinds of prayer, and perhaps being genuinely inspired by the way it seems to answer the gospel call to lose self. Their initial excitement, however, wanes when the absoluteness of that call is made actual in the sustained practice of meditation—in the fidelity to the poverty it leads to and to the regularity of returning to it daily. It was in these moments that we were often asked to moderate the simplicity, the absolute simplicity of the traditional teaching. People would say, for example, that they had reached a stage at which the discipline of the recital of the mantra was no · longer necessary for them—they were ready to be "led by the spirit" on their own. It was in these situations that discussion about meditation seemed to be most in demand—discussion that would often threaten to take the place of meditation itself. There was then only one thing to say. The act of faith that meditation demands is ever-deepening. It is a journey that begins in faith and will end in faith and it is an entirely free choice whether one follows it or not. We were not saying it was the only way. We were simply saying that if this is the way you freely choose, the teaching you choose to accept is that you recite your mantra without ceasing, until you can no longer say it. If we have to ask ourselves the question "Is it time I stopped saying it?," it is the sure sign that we must *continue* to say it.

This response to the demand for discussion about meditation in terms of "spiritual" or "incarnational" forms of prayer often led to the rejoinder that, after all, meditation is only one method of prayer and we were making exaggerated, exclusive claims for it.

The aim of our community in Montreal has always been to stress and, as far as we are able, to prove by our lives that there are no "methods of prayer." There is only prayer. There is only one prayer and this is the prayer of Jesus—not words he addresses to his Father but the overflowing plenitude of his relationship with the Father. To talk, then, of methods of prayer or of "our prayer" at all is to miss the essential Christian dimension of prayer revealed to us—that we ourselves do not know how to pray. We have to learn by following the teaching of our Master and he teaches us by taking us into the creative and liberating mystery of his prayer, the stream of love that flows between him and his Father that *is* the Spirit. "Our prayer" is simply our entering into this stream of divine love because of our realization of our incorporation with Jesus—not because we read about it and think about it, but because we *realize* it. The freedom of spirit that is the fruit and mark of prayer is due to our discovery that the stream of love we have been plunged into and that sweeps us along is the foundational principle of all reality, is Being itself.

The moment of prayer is not a moment when a technique begins to work. It is a moment of transcendence that involves us totally in the mystery of God and makes his mystery our own mystery, not something solved but life being infinitely fulfilled. The *ecstasis* of prayer is our being taken out of ourselves and inserted into the self-knowledge of the Divine Mystery. The self we have lost is found in him but no longer alienated from itself and from him by self-consciousness. The loss of self is the turning away from self. And what we turn to, though we do not know this until we turn, is the One who contains our self. The otherness of God is revealed to us in our transcendent othercenteredness.

Our letters have been an attempt to show that all renewal—whether personal renewal in Christ or monastic renewal in community—is born from an ultimate self-transcendence in the reality of the present moment. Their common point of departure is the call to each of us (a call made incarnate in each Christian) to be wholly real in the *now* that is the contemporaneity of the real God. Our modern sense of time and our distracted yearning for the next moment's consolation or amusement makes meditation difficult to see in this perspective. We can too easily be led into seeing it as a temporary vehicle to a future enlightenment and the nowness of the Christian experience gets projected into an eternal postponement, a disincarnate future. At no point in history has it been more important to listen to the tradition that reveals prayer as the progressive penetration of the present moment, as a journey ever deeper into the union of love and the progressive shedding of self that leads to that union. But, such is the risk that makes the human being free, even the tradition can teach us nothing of ultimate importance if we do not have some real light from our own experience to read it by. It is this experience that saves the tradition from ever becoming a mere memory transmitted in print, and that revitalizes it for every generation. In the personal act of faith that opens this experience to us, the tradition is invested with human relevance for all men and it is relevant because it restores us to that present moment in which we are propelled into the actuality of God.

Monastic renewal can only become mere antiquarianism if all its energies are spent in a return to historical origins. The essential understanding its scholarship can convey, however, is that the early Fathers of monasticism did not see their lives in terms of a return to the historical Jesus but rather as the wonder of their present encounter with the risen and fully alive Jesus. In this encounter they knew the freedom from history that the lordship of Jesus makes available to all men—a freedom from the individual bondages of our personal histories as well as from the species' historical enslavement to sin, to fear, ignorance, and weakness. In knowing this lordship to be the supreme present reality of man, the monastic Fathers originated a living tradition whose spirit rather than whose letter can convey the mystery to us. The tradition has to be as alive for us as it was for them and much of it has to be extracted from the raw material of our modern living. And in the same way the new creation of which Jesus is Lord must become as fresh and as liberating for us as it was for St. Paul.

What our letters try to communicate is that this knowledge of the presentness of Christ's kingdom of liberty can only ultimately come from our own encounter with the living Lord who dwells in our hearts. Monasticism and Christianity in general will be renewed for the searching needs of our own day, and will be able to share its vitally necessary heritage with humankind, only when monks return to their first responsibility—seeking God; present; now. The renewal of the monks will work like a lever in the spiritual machinery of the Christian community, inspiring others to seek God in the here and now. The chain of dependent events and spreading influence that makes up the growing Body of Christ depends upon the priority of personal commitment and the contagion of personal example. There is no shortage of books on prayer, lectures on meditation, summer courses on advanced spirituality. Our own aim, in our monastery and in the secondary means of our letters or tapes, has been the simple monastic one of leading people to the actual practice of prayer.

The difficulty that the monastic teaching and example poses for modern man is that the silence necessary for prayer must be absolute. We are all so accustomed to regarding prayer as "talking to God," "thinking about God" or "imagining God or the historical Jesus"—with all the endless variations on these themes—that it has become hard for us to be told that prayer is absolute stillness and awe in the presence of God. Of course, the pressures and distractions of modern living have made silence a theoretically desirable thing; but too often it is the silence of listening to soft music in the background or the interiorized silence where we try to hear ourselves—and, if we hear nothing, we panic and make noise. The monastic assertion that complete silence is not only the essential condition of transcendence but also a realistically possible path for ordinary men and women has to be made by practice and living example. Only then will monasticism be able to offer the courage and companionship for the journey that each person has to undertake on his or her own responsibility. Only then will it be able to reveal in the solitude of personal integrity that all humankind is summoned to full communion.

Our message in these letters was therefore a simple one to which we were constantly returning. By our experience of silence and self-integration, to which our act of faith leads us, we can begin to understand prayer not as an observation of God, or the setting of a trap for God to fall in, but as total absorption in God. To pray means to leave self behind and to find our self absorbed in God. It means that the journey from self is at the same time a penetration of the infinite mystery of God. There is no point at which we can say "we have made it." Our absorption in God involves our sharing in the infinite expansion of consciousness that is his essential nature, his love. The Christian revelation unites us to this mystery as an immediate and personal possibility not at a theological or poetical level but onotologically. The ground of our own being and the fabric of our consciousness have been themselves penetrated by the consciousness and love of Christ, whose mind and being is one with ours. The infinite mystery of God that has always been utterly beyond man and yet always contained him is now also, in person, dwelling within him.

It takes only a primary experience of prayer to convince us that this is the essential *logic* of life, the structure of being. It does not mean that all the secrets of the kingdom are revealed to us at once. But it means that we have entered into a real and personal relationship with the mystery. We have begun to turn from self, to be divinized. We have begun to put on Christ. But the great difficulty of our time is to arrive at this first experience, this first moment of truth.

It is so difficult because most of the other ways of understanding prayer are greatly weakened in their capacity to lead us to actual prayer by placing ourselves at the center of the practice. When we think about God, for example, we tend to think of him in relationship to ourselves as if we were the sun around which he orbits. All the qualities and the will we attribute to him are then emanations of our own being and desire, in direct or inverse proportion. And even at the best, when we speak of prayer as praise and adoration we do so in the assumption that the praise and adoration are "mine." In both of these approaches, of thinking of God or of praising him, we tend to be still bound by the pre-Christian *image* of God: a God separate from man and, because of this, objectified by his worshippers; unpredictable in his omnipotence, he must be placated or his attention must be continuously held. As St. Paul told Christians from the earliest days, we are no longer obliged to remain subject to these religious laws with their assumptions of inferiority and their dynamic of fear. The God who cannot be thought of or imagined can be known in love because he has brought us into the kingdom, the experience, of his dear Son. And because of this, it is not our praise or adoration that is significant. The real priase of God is the praise that rises from the mind and heart of Christ. We know this and we find ourselves centered in Him by only a brief experience of the faith of silence.

The same is true of our way of thinking of prayer as "talking to God." So often when we talk to God we are talking about ourselves: help me to do this, to be that. However altruistic the basic intention may be, the structure of the words keeps us as the center of our own consciousness. This is ironically the case for many with no religious frame of reference who see prayer only in terms of entering and finding themselves. Although they may use no words in addressing any image of God and may not be "asking for favors" with an essentially ego-centered conscious-ness, their danger of self-fixation is as great if not greater. There is no standing still on the journey, no drifting. If we become either static or "spiritually stoned," we fall back into the power of our own center of gravity, we are drawn back into the orbit of our own self-reflecting ego. It is to avoid this "fall" and to remain alert and awake on the journey that we meditate. In meditation, God the unknowable is at the center. And as we move steadily into union with that center, we come to know him by his own light. The name of this movement is love and the experience by which we know it is always a progressive loss of self and self-consciousness. But the mystery of our absorption in God is not the sum total of our own efforts. It originates in a reality of being prior to the birth of our self-consciousness: namely, our incorporation in Christ. And that is why our movement into God is the mystery of Jesus himself as he takes us with him to the Father in the Spirit.

The attempt to imagine God or Jesus is as fruitless an exercise at the time of prayer as talking to him or theologizing about him. We imagine only those who are absent. Our Christian tradition proclaims that the faith each of us has received is that God is not absent but present to us fully in the Jesus whose life lives in our heart. Our prayer, as I have said, is best understood as our awareness of God in Jesus. And so our time of prayer must be a time committed to the fullest openness we are capable of—openness to this real presence and not to the dissipation of "vain imaginings." All our images, and the phantasmagoria where thought and image are combined, derive from our own limited consciousness. All such images link us back to the central image of self, the great illusion we call the ego whose primary force is fear, the inversion of love, and which is the father of lies. It is an illusion because the true self has no image but is complete and undifferentiated consciousness. Our consciousness is limited, fractured, by the false image, the shadow of the ego, and it is set free and made whole by the light of Christ in whom there is no darkness, no separateness of being that can cast a shadow. Of Christ alone can we say that he is the image of God, the supreme Self, because of him alone can we say that he is one with the Father.

This is the message of the Christian revelation that has to be addressed to a world acutely aware of its modernity, a world built on worship of the contemporary and yet longing for the security of roots. This paradox of the modern mentality should provide a fertile soil for the paradox of Christianity, a religion that is not in the first place an historical religion but that is nevertheless rooted in the reality of the Incarnation. Its claim to be of serious relevance to men of our time is the promise of Jesus to be with us for all time, even to the end of the world. The promise can be verified in prayer and in its verification we ourselves are made truthful. It is this living Christ, the dynamic center of our prayer, who commands the attention of our world. But it is only when we know him in prayer that the promise is made and the entire written account of his historical life can make full sense and expand us as it should, in the present moment. As Kierkegaard unforgettably expressed it, "Only that past which can become present is worth remembering."

A life centered on Christ as the supreme present reality and the One who gives ultimate structure to reality is a life rooted in prayer and centered on the present moment. This present moment has, of course, its own structure. It is not a life of drifting or aimlessness but the structure is of an uncompromising simplicity, standing firm against the tendency inherent in every life toward complexity and distraction. A universal model for this structure is the monastic life, that is to say Christian life revealed in all its simplicity.

In Montreal our life is built upon the threefold synthesis of St. Benedict—*oratio* (prayer), *lectio* (reading), and *labor* (work). Four times a day we meditate together for half an hour—the "short time" of prayer suggested in the Rule. Each of these periods follows the appropriate hour of the Divine Office except for the first meditation of the morning. The Office, which we see as community *lectio*, is our way of preparing for the silence of prayer by an attentive listening to the Word in scripture.

The Benedictine synthesis of prayer, study, and work is foundational to the Christian monastic life—but the greatest of these is prayer. The central thrust of our life is toward the *oratio pura* or pure prayer that Cassian, at the outset of the monastic tradition in the West, saw as the means and end of monastic life. Insofar as we can achieve it, every other aspect of our life is aligned on this. Our *lectio* teaches us the essential prayer-fulness of concentrating away from ourselves, away from our own thoughts and responses. All monastic study essentially is sapiential rather than discursive. Just as in *lectio* our center of attention is the *word*, so in our work it is the occupation at hand. If we can use our times of work, whatever the work may involve, as moments of concentration on the act, not on the fruit of the action, we are deepening the single-mindedness that is the condition of unbroken prayer.

The personal side of community life itself is another vital preparation for prayer. In the moment of prayer our center of attention is fully focused in the Other who is Love. And in our fraternal relationships this focus is maintained because we seek to be open to the otherness of those we live with in fraternal love. Our prayer is therefore a preparation for our life in common and our community life prepares us for prayer. When we can begin to experience our life in this rhythm as wholeness and growth, then we can begin to know the wonder of what it means to say that fraternal love is the sacrament of the Divine Love in which we are all made real.

The life of a monastic community is, therefore, rooted and founded in otherness in every one of its aspects. This is at the same time the greatest contribution monasticism can offer modern humankind and one of the greatest challenges it poses to us. Although one of our profoundest needs is a reexperiencing of otherness as the finding of our lives by the losing of them, we are conditioned by the compulsive materialism and distractedness of our society to protect our lives from everything that might make us lose them. We become so threatened by the reality of others that we close in upon ourselves in fear that if we were to lose ourselves in a relationship with otherness, we would cease to exist altogether. The isolation that one can so often find in monasteries themselves grows out of the ego's fear of the loss of self, often represented as a fear of being exploited, that causes monks to retire into a private world of their own—sealed, alternative realities. In monasteries this collapse of the Christian experience of transcendence is particularly painful to see because it is above all the aim of the monastic life to prove that isolation, fear, and illusion are not inevitable. In the monastery, if anywhere, one must be able to see and meet men who are self-emptying, self-transcending disciples discovering the infinite fullness of real life together. Their lives have to overflow the limits imposed by fear. In our own way, too, we try to love the guests who visit us with that pure love whose source we are open to in our prayer and life together. By loving them we can hope to lead them to that point of confidence, that sense of their own reality that will teach them to plunge into the mystery whose center lies beyond themselves.

The monastic life and the hospitality monks have to show to all who come to them are designed to communicate the confidence necessary to let go. The experience of prayer, the entry into the silence of Jesus, is first presented to us as an invitation that it takes nerve to accept. There will always be many reasons at hand for declining or postponing the invitation. But once it has been decided to accept it, the first moment of prayer and the first self-abandoning step requires every ounce of faith we have been given. The eternal silence of God that is so attractive in poetry or theology breaks upon us in such unfamiliar otherness that it takes much love, much being loved, to continue into the silence. Our encouragement, however, is this: whatever degree of faith we have been given is sufficient to begin, and once we have begun, the love we need floods our inmost heart.

The journey of prayer is both sublime and ordinary. The ordinariness of our regularity and our mutual encouragement are the context for God's revelation of his sublimity. And a vital part of its ordinariness is our community practice of prayer in common—each of our four sessions of meditation we have in community, and it is difficult to overstress the importance of this practice. The shared silence is a self-authenticating, shared faith in God's presence among us. Learning to meditate in common is the greatest of our exercises of fraternal love because in these moments we hold open to others the most precious part of ourselves, our faith in the life-giving presence of Jesus in our heart.

The sharing of this faith demands great personal discipline as we all learn to sit absolutely still to bring together the inner and outer silence into a simple wholeness, a simple presence. The stillness that purifies us of our restlessness and distraction does so by making us aware that we are not isolated. Our very essence is *being in relationship*. Our stillness together reveals what it means to say that we are members of one body, and that Body is Christ. The fact that so much can be communicated in silence and by silence is a source of amazement. The aspect of our life that our guests find at once most inspiring and most demanding is the community's silence—the reverence in which Presence is known. ⌐

* * *

At this point, our experience, limited and incomplete as it is bound to be, has suggested to us something of great relevance to the future of Christian religious community life. The Vatican Council called religious life a "sign for the world" because it saw that the sight of men and women of faith leaving all things to follow God was of supreme value in the personal communication of the gospel. The absolute value of monastery or convent is not in witness to the private experience of God but to the universality of the experience, the reality of Jesus as a living force in the world. The monk or nun was not born in the cloister. He and she were in the world and in the world they found the reality that demanded everything they are—and to the world again they return. But they do not return *as witnesses* through their work or service. These are secondary signs of love. Their essential return is made in the deepening of their own experience of God. It has always been the teaching of the Church's tradition that the spiritual life of the members of a community should in this way be their first responsibility. But more often the reality has been that the good works in which the religious have engaged become supreme. And because the work is given priority, one of the "sacrifices" the religious makes is of his or her personal life of prayer. The crisis facing the Church's religious life has its origin in this radical distortion of the religious vocation.

It seems to me quite clear that the renewal of the religious life in lived community prayer is of supreme importance both for the Church and the world. There are things that must be said in sincere faith and with real persuasion that perhaps only monks or religious can say, and if these are not said, not witnessed to, society grows deformed. If they are to be said again, not as boring, traditional platitudes but as *words* of a living tradition, it will require a generous and selfless reevaluation of the way religious pray and work. The connection between the two has to be rediscovered as one of the most urgent priorities we face because the way we pray radically shapes the way we work and witness to the utterness and presentness of the love of Christ. If our prayer is not centered in that love and our lives not centered in our prayer, how can our work be aligned on Him?

Our own thinking on this question has been enriched by feedback from many of the religious that these talks and letters have already reached. We know that they are a drop in an ocean with unpredictable tides. The rise and fall of monastic life in the Church is not, for all that, totally dependent on uncontrolled forces. It rises with faith and falls when faith fails. It has often not been from religious that my own faith in the monastic life in the future has been strengthened as much as from the countless lay people of all traditions and backgrounds who have declared the value, for them, of a community committed to prayer, as its clear and first priority.

However, some people on reading the letters have found them uncompromising, not to say arrogant. They seemed to them too self-confident, and to suggest that the spiritual insights they contain, such as they are, are put forward as the only insights there are. I hope there is not too much truth in these reactions and, by way of mitigation rather than defense, I would say that whatever their style or tone their doctrine has grown out of commitment and living. The words are not unrelated to experience. The words have been burned into the heart.

These letters are a small part of a vast tradition of Christians writing to each other to share their joy in their knowledge of their Lord and to encourage each other to persevere on the way of prayer that is this knowledge. The letters of St. Paul that crown this tradition were an urgent, even desperate, attempt to communicate to the first Christians what we have always had to recommunicate to each other. If his letters convey to us the incredible richness of the mystery of Christ, it is because they speak from his own lived response to that mystery. They have become the model for all Christian witness—a model we stand in urgent need of rediscovering—showing that authority comes from conviction and conviction from experience. If I seem to be intolerant of other ways it is not because I wish to dismiss other ways or traditions. It is only because the faith I have in this monastic way and tradition is a loving and urgent one.

JOHN MAIN, OSB

March 1982
The Benedictine Priory
1475 Pine Avenue West
Montreal, Quebec, Canada H3G 1B3

Letter One (DECEMBER 1977)

On September 28, 1977, Brother Laurence and I flew from London to Montreal. At Mirabel Airport we were met by Bishop Leonard Crowley, whose initiative had brought us to make the first monastic foundation in this city. For six weeks we stayed in the rectory of a parish church as we waited for the house we were in the process of buying to be freed from the last formalities of sale. It was an old French-Canadian farmhouse situated in Notre Dame de Grace, a quiet residential district about fifteen minutes from the center of the city. The house had grown with the increasing prosperity of succeeding generations of the Decarie family, one of the familes who had first settled in Quebec three hundred years ago. But the old grandeur of the house had given way to loose windows and falling ceilings when we walked into it the day after our arrival. For several months its restoration was a labor of love that occupied the whole community and many of our first guests.

As a result of our tapes and people who had visited our center in London, we found a meditation group already formed and meeting each week. Soon after we had finally moved into the house on December 6, this group began to meet here and so formed the nucleus of all the groups that formed around us later. It seemed natural to keep the structure of these meetings the same as the one that had evolved at the London center: an introductory talk, music, a half hour meditating in silence together, the raising of questions or a discussion. The existence of this group was a great help, however, in establishing from the outset that the first priority and center of our work is meditation, not just talking about meditation.

In these early days of our community I accepted a few invitations to talk about our work. In Boston and Montreal I spoke to religious communities and in Kingston, Ontario, to a regional meeting of university chaplains. The people who came to meditate with us were, from the first, of every age and type and included many non-Christians.

December 10, 1977

Dearest Friends,

Greetings in the Lord. This letter is to wish you every happiness and blessing for Christmas and in the New Year.

Please forgive the delay in sending you this first newsletter from Montreal. On arrival in Montreal we discovered that a difficulty had arisen over the purchase of our house as the Court had to agree to the contract of sale. But now that we are in the house, we can meet regularly for our meditation and the Office.

Since arriving, I have given weekends of retreat to various groups expressing interest in the Benedictine Community. In addressing a meeting of university chaplains, I tried to express and share my own conviction that the preeminent need our world has is for men and women who can speak about and communicate Christianity out of their own experience. And that there is no other way to meet this need that is not the way of personal commitment and personal fidelity to the path of prayer.

The Chaplains were from all Christian denominations and they all shared the same concern over their role in the university: were they to be counselors or spiritual leaders? I thought that their dilemma was in many ways the common choice facing all Christians today. Every one of us is called to be a full person, fully realized in the light of the power of the Spirit continuously springing up into life eternal in our heart, fully mature, fully human. And when the Spirit is set free in us, set free of the constricting bonds of our ego, our self-fixation, it pervades every faculty and fiber of our being. Then we become the witnesses we are called to be—witnessing with our own quality of life and our own fearless power to love to the essential, Christian, and truly human experience of the transcendent Spirit of Jesus living in the center of our being, where he holds us and all things in being. In that experience we find our own inner coherence, our harmony with others and with the forces within us and without us. The sense of our coherence creates the confidence we need to leave thought of self, self-consciousness, behind and to live no longer for ourselves but for Him. There is only one Teacher and that is the Lord Jesus, the Teacher within. But in our union with him we are summoned to mediate his teaching, which is only his love—to make his union with all men fully conscious, fully alive.

I am sure that you do not need me to remind you that in order to do this we have to have seriously undertaken the pilgrimage of prayer. This is not an abstract, theoretical undertaking. To make this pilgrimage we have to put our prayer first, and this in a very practical way. In planning our day we must see to it that we leave a time and space for our meditation—a time and space that will come to be more and more what holds our day and indeed our life in shape and on course. And we must come to see this not as our own time but as God's time.

The night before last I addressed a meeting of sisters from the Diocese of Montreal on the eve of the Feast of the Immaculate Conception. I spoke to them on what I think is the essential meaning of Mary and indeed of all those men and women whom God has raised up as signs of the holiness to which all men and women are called. The meaning is, above all, in her being a model of simplicity: a simplicity of consciousness, simplicity of heart, simplicity of faith. With this condition of simplicity—"a condition that demands not less than everything"—there comes that directness of encounter with the power of God within us that deepens and fulfils us. The process is continuous because there is no end to the power of God. And therefore no end to our capacity for love.

Our task is to persevere—not grudgingly or self-importantly, but with simple faith and self-renewing love. The figure of Mary is a central one in our understanding of Christmas. Above all, she is a great example of interiority with a direct meaning for each of us. Just as she carried the human Christ within her, so we must bear and worship Christ in our own hearts, remembering that he is just as truly present within us as he was bodily present in his mother.

Mary in the gospels has another meaning for us: her silence is both the medium and the response to the presence of Jesus within us. The true silence of our meditation is creative and fertile. As it deepens and grows, so does the presence and power of the risen Christ expand the kingdom of love in our heart.

Our task is to be silent, to be still, and to allow his transforming presence to emerge within us, out of the living, creative center of our being.

Please keep all of us here in Montreal in your hearts. We shall remember you all as we offer our Midnight Mass together: In Him, Through Him and With Him.

With much love,

John Main, OSB

Letter Two (FEBRUARY 1978)

Our first Christmas in Montreal had required a fair amount of improvisation, but the simplicity of it all had made us happy and it was marked by many gestures of kindness and generosity from people welcoming us here. The house began to take shape week by week. Most of our decorating efforts were devoted to the meditation room, formerly the two large music rooms of the house, light-filled and high-ceilinged.

We were able to meditate in it for the third meeting of our weekly group in February. The group was growing steadily with serious newcomers and represented a good crosssection of Montreal society. At any one meeting there would be middle-aged people who had started to meditate a year or two before with TM, sudents returning from a yoga retreat, businessmen and housewives, and often our most open and welcoming parish priest. The group had grown to about twenty by the time we sent out our second newsletter and we were already thinking of starting a second group as large as our space made comfortable. We had always thought the ideal size of a group is about twelve but the number of free evenings in a week made this difficult to realize either here or in London.

We were happy to see that people felt easy about joining us for the regular meditation sessions of the Community. At this stage there were three sessions: at 6.30 A.M. with the Morning Office and Eucharist, at noon with the Midday Office, and after Vespers at 5.15 P.M.

There was little time to think of new publications as yet, although our experience in Montreal was shaping a new theology for us that was always developing and that found expression in the newsletters. We were glad, though, to know that our tapes, which themselves had grown out of our work in London, had found good distributors. In North America they were taken care of by N.C.R. of Kansas City and in England by the Grail of Pinner. Encouraging news of the English meditation groups we had left behind continued to arrive. The Grail itself had started a small group of about three regular members and this was soon to flourish and produce other groups. Several of the hundreds who had visited the London center felt ready to undertake the challenge of starting their own group as soon as they had felt for themselves the deep support that meditating with a community can give. Small or large, these groups had begun to meet regularly to support one another in their fidelity to their twice-daily meditations. Our letters to these groups, like our talks in Montreal, continued to put the message in as simple and direct a way as we could. To meditate required *faith* —fidelity to each morning and evening meditation.

Our life in Montreal was aiming to be a witness to this message. We had set our priority on a life based firmly on our regular periods of meditation together. Whatever developed in the way of groups, or the opportunity to share our faith in monasticism with others, we would respond to as generously as we could. Meanwhile, we received constant support and encouragement from Bishop Crowley, who always prayed with us when he came to see us. And the word of our presence continued to circulate personally rather than by publicity.

On my previous visit to Montreal in April to arrange our arrival, I had been asked to give a weekly series of talks to the parents of a large school here. These were given January through March, more than once dramatized by snowstorms, but they gave the opportunity to explain our purpose over a long period to a sympathetic group.

On Shrove Tuesday, I spoke to the Faculty of Religious Studies at McGill University and met there some who would become great supporters of our community and its work. Brother Laurence resumed his theological studies at the University of Montreal, managing to schedule them so as to allow his full participation in our community life.

Another frequent participant in our life was an elderly German-Canadian who came to us in our earliest days to greet us as fellow Benedictines. He and his wife had been Oblates of Mount Saviour for twenty years and were close friends of its founder, Damasus Winzen. We were little aware in these early days how significant that connection with Mount Saviour was to be.

February 2, 1978
Feast of the Presentation

My Dearest Friends,

Greetings in the Lord.

First, we must thank you for all the letters we received in response to our first newsletter. Please forgive us for not yet answering them all personally. We were delighted to hear news of you and encouraged, above all, to learn that you remain faithful to your meditation.

We started our first group with just six people—as you can imagine, it was a memorable evening for us. As the text for the first talk, I took the words of Jesus in the Gospel of Mark: "Anyone who wishes to be a follower of mine must leave self behind; he must take up his cross and come with me" (Mark 8:34). They are the words that really sum up all we have to say at any time and in any place about what it means to follow Jesus, to be on the pilgrimage.

Yesterday evening we had our third meeting of the group and our first session in our new meditation room. At this point I am about halfway through a series of talks here and what I have been trying to say so far is that Christianity is, above all, the communication to us of the power of God. And it is an *act* of communication, not a hypothesis or a "nice idea." It is a real and continuous act that reveals a real and personal relationship at the very center of our life and being. Now, every act of communication in which we can participate must have its own medium—there must be a means by which we can receive what is being communicated to us. The means of God's communication of his power to us is, everywhere and always, the person of Jesus. Jesus, who is the image of the invisible God, is also the son of man, our brother. Because he incorporates us into his person, we are able to receive that communication from God—the communication of his power that is the experience, the knowledge, and the receiving of his love. In receiving this communication (which is prayer), we are brought to a real knowledge of ourselves because we are brought to a real awareness of God as the source of our being, and also, in our incorporation in Jesus, the end of the pilgrimage that is the characteristic of our being human. In my end is my beginning.

Another way of saying this is to say that Christianity is the *experience* of the power—what the gospel calls the *dynamos*—of God. But it is *experience* in a special sense. It is something greater than the merely three-dimensional experience of pleasure. It is the transcendent experience of joy. Anyone who loves another person for his or her own sake and delights in that person's unique being will know what this experience entails. And, indeed, only they can because "the man who does not love is still in the realm of death" (1 John 3:15). The Christian experience of the love of God in Jesus is a transcendent experience, an experience of joy. But this does not mean that it is not a reality of the present, rooted in us as we are at the present moment. What the whole Christian mystery proclaims is the meeting of our "world" and the "world" of God in the person of Jesus — the same person of Jesus who calls us into himself through the Spirit he has given us. And so, the power of God is a power within us — in our hearts — and yet it is also a power utterly beyond us — the transcendent power of the God whom the eye of man cannot see nor his mind imagine. But this is the difference that the coming of Jesus has made for all mankind: his redemptive love is a continuous, insuperable power that opens up for us the possibility of entering the experience of the power of God — through him, for he is the Way.

This can tell us something about the nature of true Christian community. A group of Christians who meet together to meditate, to pray, to worship is not, then, just a mere social gathering. It is a group aware of its power: a power that arises from the transcendent reality of the presence of the Lord Jesus in their midst. The purpose of their meeting is, before anything else, to attend to the reality of this presence, to deepen their silent receptivity to it, to make it (what it already is) the supreme reality of their lives. So, each member of the group is other-centered, turned away from him or herself toward the living Lord. And the group then becomes truly a community — like that described to us at the end of the second chapter of Acts: "A sense of awe was everywhere . . . all whose faith had drawn them together held everything in common . . . with unaffected joy."

The Christian group, then, must always be aware of its ultimate meaning being beyond itself. The social, cultural, or ceremonial form of the group must never become something to be preserved or, above all, something to be possessed: all truly Christian response requires detachment and it is this very detachment that helps us to enjoy externals while never ceasing to concentrate on the essential reality. And, of course, the reality is the transcending reality—the power of the risen Lord Jesus. All this is, of course, so obvious, but it was just this proclamation of the essential liberty of the spirit by Jesus that seemed such a threat to the Pharisees. And our tendency, too, is often to opt for the static security of an established order, what we know and what we feel safe with. The tragedy of such an option is that it does not even allow us to remain static: we go into decline because we have opted to evade the only real security there is—the rock of Christ, the *dynamos* of God, the glorious liberty of the children of God. Our glory and liberty as Christians is just that we have been enabled to make this positive option, to turn away from ourselves and our anxiety and what has enabled us to do so is that we have been turned around by Jesus.

This "turning around" is the subject of a talk I am giving at McGill University on Shrove Tuesday. What I will be saying then is that by becoming man God has turned toward us in Jesus. Jesus showed himself to us and in so doing revealed the Father to us: "Anyone who has seen me has seen the Father," as John's gospel tells us (John 14:9). But this is the beginning of the Christian mystery, not the end of it. It is where we begin to enter the mystery as we are called to do because in turning toward us, in revealing God to us, Jesus has presented us with the opportunity, and indeed the responsibility, of turning toward him. We are not able to open our hearts to him, revealing the power of love in our hearts turned toward him.

And this is our way. Just as Jesus is the medium of God's revelation to man, so we, as his Body, the Church, are the medium of his revelation to the world. As I have so often said to you before, Christianity depends for its authenticity upon our witness. We have to proclaim the Good News out of our own experience. In the first chapter of his gospel, St. Luke speaks of basing the "authentic knowledge" of his book on "the original eyewitnesses and servants of the gospel." To understand the relevance of this remark we should listen to what St. Paul says in chapter 9 of 1 Corinthians: "Am I not an apostle? Did I not see Jesus our Lord?" Neither Paul nor Luke had known the historical Jesus. But what they are both proclaiming is the profound Christian reality that the "Way" is not merely a historical tradition but is something much greater: our own lived experience of the present reality of the risen Lord Jesus, the Christ.

The wonder is that this is our Way. In Luke's narratives there is the motif of Christ's journey to Jerusalem. Indeed, the whole of his account of Jesus' ministry is framed as his progress toward the holy city, his being en route to his great priestly destiny, which was that moment in his life when he was to burst the bonds of every limitation implicit in his incarnation—to become, as St. Paul tells us, "life-giving spirit" (1 Cor. 15:45). In Luke's account, the sign of a person's response to Jesus as he journeyed to Jerusalem was whether or not he or she turned around, changed direction, and followed him.

During his ministry, the "Way" was the journey Jesus followed as his pilgrimage through love and suffering to his Father. But after the perfection of his love in the suffering of the Cross, he reached the goal of his pilgrimage and was glorified in his return to the Father's right hand. And so it is that in chapter 14 of his gospel St. John tells us that the Way now is the person of Jesus himself.

Christian prayer, then, has the essentially dynamic quality of the mystery of Jesus himself because it is an encounter and entry into the person of Jesus, who is the way to the Father. The Christian pilgrimage is a turning, a conversion, a following of Christ and a journey with Christ. It is never complacent or self-satisfied. And its essential insight is that our full meaning lies beyond ourselves. Salvation, within this terminology, is *being on the Way*, being turned toward the dynamic power of Jesus and being taken up in him to the Father. Salvation is entering the kingdom of heaven that is within us.

One of the great perils of the pilgrimage is that we talk so much about it and so cleverly *imagine* ourselves on it that we actually fail to tread it, to put one foot in front of the other. I have spoken to you of this danger often enough. It is the *pax perniciosa*, mere religiosity or "holy floating." We are all in continuous need of that quality that St. Paul speaks of in 1 Thessalonians (chapter 1)—the quality of *hippomone*, sometimes translated as patience, sometimes as endurance, but best of all, it seems to me, as fortitude. This is the courage to keep on the Way with growing fidelity to our twice-daily meditation—times in the day when we quite explicitly put everything aside so that we may enter the journey of the Lord with our full attention. Let no one deceive you into thinking that this explicit "work" is not necessary. Of course, we are always on the Way, always journeying with him. It is the condition of all creatures and all creation. But we are called to a full, mature, and personal awareness of it. And just as he stood aside from his ministry of healing, teaching, and preaching to be alone with his Father, wholly turned toward his presence at the center of his being, so too must we follow in this Way. The Gospels clearly testify to his practice of withdrawing from his active ministry and the crowds that followed him to pray in silence and solitude. But this was in addition to the normal religious practice of his day he would have followed, of the three regular periods of prayer during the day. The practical, daily structure of his life was, then, provided by his faithful commitment to prayer.

So, too, our life. The structure of our life must be based on our regular, silent attentiveness to the source of our life—if we are to accept that "fullness of life" Jesus offers. After all that one can say about prayer and however wonderful the mystery seems to our mind, it comes down to this: fidelity to our twice-daily meditation and, within the time of meditation, complete fidelity to the word—the mantra that leads us on the Way. The beauty of the gospels, the delight of creation, the concerns of our life—everything must be placed on the altar of the living sacrifice of praise we offer by saying our mantra. By saying it to the exclusion of all thought and imagination we will be led into a depth of silence on the other side of all distraction. In this silence, Jesus, the Word, is rooted in our hearts; we are made one with him; we journey with him to the Father.

I will end the talk at McGill as I must end this letter—by reminding you that for a full, balanced, and enriching Christian life we must experience the fullness of the Christ-event. That fullness is found in the mystery of the death and Resurrection of Jesus. It is to be found in the community of those who accept him as Lord and Savior—his Church. And it is found in our hearts: in the presence of his living and life-giving spirit within us.

So let us live our lives to the full, followers of the Way in his Church, bringing his fullness of life to all mankind.

Peace in the Lord,

John Main, OSB

Letter Three (APRIL 1978)

A s regards the weather, our first winter in Montreal was a very
pleasant surprise. Instead of the predicted blizzards and frostbite,
we delighted in crisp, blue skies and bright, cold sunlight week after
week. The work on the inside of the house was nearing completion and
we looked ahead to being able to start on the roof and front gallery.

Our liturgy was able to develop in tune with our experience and
formed a response to the actual personal situation that grew week by
week. Having our clear priority in meditation made this development
more natural and flexible, not less so, and it pleased us to see that the
growth was human enough to be able to find a real place for children.
This was no doubt made easier by our small numbers — it never seemed
necessary to discuss or become self-conscious about the liturgical
expression of the journey we were making together. And even our
restricted space brought the great symbols of the liturgical season into
sharper focus and a more personal meaning.

The growing number of guests from Canada, the States, and soon
from overseas helped to ensure that we remained open to the outside
forces that also conditioned our growth. We were hampered here by
lack of space, to remedy which we rented an apartment for the lay
community a few minutes' walk from the house. We were now able to
take two or three guests at a time.

Our work centered more and more on teaching the tradition of
meditation we ourselves were following and sharing our experience of
it. The weekly group had continued to grow and we had therefore set
aside Monday night for an introductory session, with the same structure
as before, and Tuesday night for those who had been coming to us for
some time and had begun to meditate regularly in their own lives. We
also started a group for priests at the request of several in the diocese.
The response to this was not great but a solidly committed core of about
seven priests soon formed and met faithfully each week to meditate
together. As we talked together afterward in the months ahead, the
group began to focus in on what it saw as the most pressing problem:

How were they to communicate what they had experienced not only to their parishioners, but to their fellow priests? At this stage the answer was not clear and they faithfully continued to root themselves in the daily fidelity of their meditation, but within a year the impulse to communicate their experience was seeking real expression.

Bishop Crowley continued to support and encourage us in these days of *enracinement* and visited regularly to pray with us and meet the new members of the community.

About this time we invited a group of local businessmen and academics who had helped us since our arrival to form a committee to advise us on plans we had for finding a larger property. It was to be a long search for the right place and the project grew in urgency as time passed. The delay, however, gave us time to consider more deeply what were the implications of the development of our work for our vision of the monastic life in a modern world. It was clear we were living a more contemplative life-style than that of the English Benedictine Congregation, with its emphasis on the apostolates of schoolteaching and parochial work. Yet even as we nurtured the specifically monastic growth of the community, the demand to share our experience with a widening range of people also grew.

Not surprisingly, we asked ourselves: What was the monastic witness to a modern world? How was the prayer of monks to find its full meaning for others? From all sides we heard complaints that the Church was failing to teach with both relevance and authority. And from America, Europe, and Africa we heard of an attempt to recover the central experience of Christianity, the knowledge of the indwelling presence of Christ, as the basis for that relevance and authority. It was here that a truly alive and contemporary monasticism had to find its meaning in proving the experience possible and self-communicating. I heard the same kind of concerns expressed at a meeting of lay directors of the Spiritual Exercises I addressed. Among these was the same search for authority and genuine experience. But how were they to gain the experience unless they allowed themselves to be taught? (No one can teach what he has not learned for himself.) They needed to learn the essential teaching that there is only one Teacher and the experience we all seek is to know him. Partly in response to these discussions and partly to letters we were receiving from the English groups, we took all this up in our next newsletter.

April 25, 1978

My Dearest Friends,

Greetings in the Lord!
I am hoping that this will reach you in time for your celebration of the great Feast of Pentecost. This is the time when

the whole Easter mystery really find its completion. From Christmas onward, through Lent and the three days of Easter itself, it is as if we are reliving the past, participating in the life and growth of Jesus up to the moment of his human fulfillment; as if we are learning how to identify our lives with his. We, too, have to lay down our lives and turn away from self to God. But after the Ascension there is that strange liturgical interval when it seems as if our identification, our union with Jesus, can go no further—until the day of Pentecost, when the fire of the Holy Spirit touched the hearts of the Apostles as it touches ours. And then we know why Jesus said he had to go in order to send the Spirit—to bring the Father's plan, the work of union to completion in the here and now. Pentecost gathers together all of the mystery of Easter and realizes it in us at the present moment. From now on there is only one thing to do to fully awaken to this living mystery within us as a present reality. This is the work, the pilgrimage of our meditation.

Holy Week was a time of much grace and happiness for us here. The culmination of the week was the baptism of a friend of ours who has been meditating with us since we arrived in Montreal. On Easter night, before as many people as we could accommodate, he was baptized and confirmed at our Vigil service. And then, as at all our ceremonies, we were able to meditate together in silence. During the last weeks I have been talking to various groups about our community and our work. As you know, this really comes down to the practical way we try to live the Christian tradition of prayer as a monastic community: to follow the "Way," to pursue the pilgrimage. I had in particular a very rewarding evening with about twenty directors of the Ignatian Spiritual Exercises. I was asked to share something of the Benedictine monastic understanding of the role of a "spiritual director."

I began by saying that the very idea of a "director" originates in that of the monastic "spiritual father," and the way this ancient Christian tradition developed can tell us something of the needs of the Church today. The communication of the gospel and the Christian experience has always had to be a personal communication because the mystery itself is in the fullest sense a personal one: the person of the Lord Jesus whose fulfilled personhood already now involves and contains ours. The monastery, in particular, has always been a place where the wonder of this personal mystery is realized and incarnated in a special way through fraternal love and what St. Benedict called the "mutual obedience" of the community. In this way the monastery is a kind of microcosm of the Christian community at large and a place where the essential priorities of the Christian response are so arranged as to stand out in clear relief. Cassian, from whom Benedict derived much of his vision of the monastic life, also knew that the handing on of the tradition of prayer within the community was necessarily a personal communication. "Apart from the fact," he wrote in the *Institutes*, "that a life which is tested, refined, and purified is only found in a few people there is also the advantage that a man is more thoroughly instructed and formed by the example of one person . . . rather than from too many." His point here is not that the teacher gives an experience or assumes the individual's personal responsibility for commitment to the pilgrimage and perseverance on it. But the teacher helps to concentrate the novice's resources, to bring unity and one-centeredness to his quest, to save him from dispersing himself among "many and strange doctrines." The monastic tradition, like the Christian tradition in which it is a central stream, is passed on through books and institutions, but it does not come alive until it is regenerated in the communication of a personal encounter. But this encounter must be fully personal, fully conscious. Where we have so often lost the vitality of the tradition is in thinking of the teacher or "spiritual director" as someone who will always be there to absolve us of our personal commitment to mature growth in spirit. If a teacher is there to lead, encourage, and simplify, it is only in order that the disciple may as quickly as possible come to that transcendence of self that will enable him, in his turn, to be a channel of the love and power of the Lord for others. The teacher is a stepping stone.

The essential points to remember about the commitment to which we are called are those that tell us that "we do not even know how to pray" and that to enter the Kingdom we must become "as little children." These are essential Christian, practical truths. Taking them absolutely seriously is a permanent challenge to us. We have to realize that when we talk about "our prayer" we are really talking about our diposing ourselves for the full liberation of the life of the Spirit within us, which is the prayer of Jesus and his vital connection with the Father. This is why we pray to the degree that we turn away from ourselves, from the possessive self-consciousness and trivial distractedness of everything we sum up as ego. That this really does mean everything is the demand it makes. It is summed up in the old monastic saying, "A monk is only truly praying when he does not know that he is praying." If this sounds like annihilation, it is only because it is a description of the unified consciousness of transcendence—a condition of complete simplicity that demands no less than everything. The difference between childlikeness and childishness is the essential challenge. We have also to realize that the "kingdom" that the childlike enter is one that demands the *ascesis* of deepening simplicity at the core of our being, where, far from being annihilated, we are fully, wonderfully restored to ourselves. For the first time in our lives we know the wonder of our being, the beauty of life, the centrality of love.

The call Jesus makes to "leave self behind" is easily muted, compromised, or postponed—perhaps most often postponed; we are "too busy," or the work we are doing is just at this moment "too important." It is easier to drift in reverie rather than to "stay awake and pray." It is easier, too, to opt for the restless complexity of self-conscious reflection rather than for the still, truly alert simplicity of being who we are, where we are. And this is precisely where the encouragement, support, and confident up-building of a teacher and community are needed—the two being intimately connected in the life of the novice, just as Jesus and the Church are in the life of every Christian, the supreme model on which the Christian life is based. What these give is the great religious quality of steadiness, rootedness. The word *guru* means "one who is steady and the pilgrimage demands a constant balance, an insertion into the reality of our own existence, a centrality of commitment as our first priority. The teacher within community is only the one who points to this with constancy and directness. He does not talk for Jesus. Jesus talks for himself. But he can help us to the essential prerequisite of listening which is silence. To do this we have to be truly disciples of the Lord, that is, to have discipline; and the teacher's role is to lead people to a mature choice to pursue their pilgrimage with discipline. He is not there to teach or communicate an experience because that is in the Lord's disposal. Rather, he is one who can help us to remain serious, to be faithful and to avoid the self-centeredness that delays or stifles growth in wholeness. It is Jesus who is the exemplar of this, and his authority as a teacher was rooted in his humility. The humblest of his sayings was not, as the Pharisees and High Priest thought, an expression of his egoism but a testimony to his complete other-centeredness: the Father and I are one.

Just as the center of Jesus' consciousness is his Father, so our center of consciousness must be Jesus. When we have turned wholly towards him as the central reality of our life to which everything else is relative, then his full, unified consciousness dawns within us. In our loving union with him at the center, and consequently at all levels of our being, we know him as the One Teacher — we know it though it is beyond knowledge because, as St. Paul proclaims to us, "We have the mind of Christ." There is the one Lord and he is the only teacher, the *sadguru*. "You need no other teacher, but learn all you need to know from his initiation, which is real and no illusion. As he taught you, then, dwell in him." (1 John 2:27).

One of the great values of St. Benedict's vision of the Christian life is that of the *via media*, the middle way. Indeed, the Rule could be summed up in the three words of one of its central phrases — *ne quid nimis* (Ch. 64) — nothing in excess. This entails the renunciation of all fanaticism, social or religious. Benedict's insight was a very deep one, though expressed very simply. The essence of fanaticism, he saw, was the ego's terror of losing itself in the other and its desperate attempt to defend itself against the intrusion of what R. D. Laing calls the "implosion" of reality. Instead, Benedict put before his monks in simple, concrete terms the way to grow fully open to that reality; namely, the commitment to the steady perseverance and fidelity of prayer as a daily renewal. The very language he used contains the essence of the visions: *via media*, like "meditation," arises from the word *medius*, the middle or center. It is there that we have to be rooted, it is there our pilgrimage leads us, it is there we truly are. The word *meditare* itself, our word "meditate," also expresses the way to follow this path of centrality. Its original meaning is to turn something over again and again, to repeat. It is, as you know, by the faithful recitation of our mantra that we are led and rooted into the center of our being.

Until you have seriously undertaken this pilgrimage and made the first of many commitments to stay on it, I suppose this sounds like an unlikely doctrine despite the authority of the tradition behind it. It is, of course, a paradox that our "inward renewal" depends on stillness and our vitality and creativity on steadiness. Our contemporary culture flatly denies it. But this is only one facet of the multifaceted diamond, a reflection of the central paradox of the Christian experience, which is the Paschal mystery itself. And although this is a hard saying, it is one that strikes a chord in us all. This is perhaps why those who meditate are those who have experienced that what is ultimately enervating and dissatisfying is distraction and restlessness. The evasion of our own inner stillness and inner reality—which is no less than the abiding personal presence of Jesus, our true self—creates anxiety where there should be delight and liberty, creates the prison of our false personae where there should be the expanse of our real identity. And this evasion is the result of fear: a fear both of otherness and ourselves that creates both violence toward others and rejection of ourselves.

The wonder of the Christian revelation is of the unity of being: the union of Jesus with his Father, of ourselves with Jesus. And so, when in our meditation we turn away from the restless ego of our fears, desires, and concerns and turn instead towards the Other, we truly find ourselves in Jesus and do so at the source of our being, the love of the Father. This pilgrimage demands courage to turn away from self; but there is no discovery, no arrival, unless, in Paul Tillich's phrase, we cross the "frontier of our own identity." This is as true for you and me as it is for the whole Church today. Until people, either individually or in community, have transferred their center of consciousness out of themselves, they have not found themselves. You will see that the *via media*, the middle way of meditation, is no compromise!

Because of this and because the depth of commitment to which we are called is absolute, meditation is, quite literally, the prayer of faith. And if there is one concept we should get clearly in focus, it is the real meaning of faith. I have spoken to many of you before about the fundamental importance of our personal response to the summons of Jesus, of our turning with a whole and unfragmented consciousness toward the mystery of his indwelling Spirit. I have said to you that as real and powerful as that presence is in our hearts, and as wonderful as the transformation is that it can effect, it will not impose itself on us by force—because it is Love. It will not break through the doors of our hearts. We must open our hearts to it. The wonderful beauty of prayer is that the opening of our hearts is as natural as the opening of a flower. Just as a flower opens and blooms when we let it be, so if we simply *are*, if we become and remain silent, then our hearts cannot but open: the Spirit cannot but pour through into our whole being. It is this we have been created for. It is what the Spirit has been given to us to bring about.

This is the real meaning of faith: openness, perseverance in wakefulness, commitment to the pilgrimage. The word for faith (*pistis*) so common in the gospel sayings of Jesus nowhere in his teachings meant "belief" or "conviction." It carries instead the sense of "trust," "faithfulness," personal loyalty. To follow Jesus was not merely to have an intellectual understanding about him but to experience his personal revelation and the dimension of spirit his person opened up for us—to experience this at the center of our lives to the point of union with him and so ultimately with the Father. "He who believes [has *pistis*] in me, believes not in me but in him who sent me" (John 13:44). The openness and steadiness of this faith in Jesus leads us to the transcendence of every human limitation separating us from the Father's love, the source and goal of our being. No one approaches the Father except through Jesus. He is the Way. But we do not enter onto the way except through faith. Once we have entered upon it it will progressively draw more and more of our being into itself. It will seem as if it is integrating and unifying us simply in order to possess us and fill us more perfectly. Out of this central Christian experience flows the abundance of joy and hope proclaimed by the gospel and a rootedness in ourselves and the reality of the redemptive power of love in human life. It does not demand merely our emotional or our intellectual faculties but the whole person offered as a living sacrifice in the praise of heart and mind. Through the wonder of this wholeness a complete revolution is effected in us: "When anyone is united to Christ there is a new world; the old order has gone and a new order has already begun" (2 Cor. 5:17).

As the new world reveals itself more and more fully we begin to see the mystery as truly a *personal* one. Once a Christian has entered upon this pilgrimage he or she becomes a vital force through which the personal communication of Jesus is made. Each one of us is summoned to participate in this work of union. If we say, "This is too much for me" or "I don't know what to do," we are evading the call. All we have to do is to accept the gift we have been given: the gift of the life of the risen Lord, which can transform us and renew us in our turning toward him with our whole consciousness fully awake to its power. The courage we need for this is the courage to become truly silent, deeply unified. It is our mantra, taking us beyond the constrictions of language and imagination, that leads us into the unbounded reality of the Lord Jesus. Our twice-daily meditations and during these our absolute fidelity to the mantra as the one occupation of our mind and heart—this is our lifeline with the center to which we are travelling and out of which flows the abundant power of love to remain steady on the way of centrality. And the center where all lines converge is Jesus.

The wonderful thing about the relationship we now have between our community here and all the groups and friends in America, Europe, and Africa is that it is renewed daily in meditation, in the pilgrimage we share to the center. Its freshness does not depend on novelty but on our ever deeper penetration into the reality of the Kingdom into which the pilgrimage of the one word leads us more completely. The wonder and power of that reality manifests itself with greater and greater generosity.

This letter has been quite long and sometimes quite elaborate. Let me end by reminding you that nothing can be said about prayer that can at the same time describe its utter fullness and its utter simplicity. I suggest that you now forget most of what I have said to you except the two words "simplicity" and "faith" — and both of these are summed up in the practice of the mantra, which will allow the Spirit to guide you. I do not suggest that the simplicity is easy to reach or the faith easy to maintain. But let me remind you again that our wholehearted openness to love is the condition to which you and I and every human being is called. It is the meaning and purpose of our lives. It demands a great deal, but in the end we will find that all we have lost are our limitations.

We keep you all in our heart every day and wish you every blessing and the full joy in the Lord to which we are all called.

With much love,

John Main, OSB

Letter Four (SEPTEMBER 1978)

E arly in May I gave some retreats in California. It is a part of the world where talks on meditation are no novelty but also one that finds the essential qualities of meditation, seriousness and fidelity very challenging. In this society of entertainment and spiritual eclecticism, but marked, too, by so much genuine searching for a true experience of absolute value, it seemed to me that the monastic witness of the kind we were making in Montreal was of supreme importance — simply to prove to a culture built to such an extent on "conditional discipleship" that only the *absolute* commitment can bring the liberation they seek and so often do not find.

While I was there I heard that the Abbot of our founding monastery in London was planning his visit to us that month. On my return I found that Brother Laurence had prepared a program for his visit that would introduce him to a wide spectrum of our work and acquaintance while also allowing him to participate in our round of prayer and worship. With us he visited our neighboring Benedictine and Cistercian brethren of the city and he spoke with the Archbishop and Bishop Crowley. All his engagements confirmed the impression he took back to share with the Abbey that our foundation was finding its roots here far more surely and deeply than any of us had anticipated. It seemed evident we would have to reconsider our original three-year trial period, as this would unnecessarily delay our growth. It was important for it to be seen that our commitment here, despite the uncertain political situation and our small numbers, was serious. His visit gave us the chance to discuss the way we would best follow the line of monastic development we had begun. Apart from the deepening contemplative orientation (we had by now built a fourth meditation period into the day, after Compline), which was leading us into a monasticism very different from the London community's, our opening a novitiate or moving our location would be tiresomely complicated if we were waiting for the approval of the community in England at each step. We agreed, therefore, that as soon as the right moment came we would transfer our monastic association from England. The evident momentum we had gained and the enthusiasm we had encountered made it a decision as amicable as it was, we hoped, selfless. We had to wait now and see when this important move should be made.

We had other monastic guests that summer, from the London monastery and from Washington D.C., and a six-week visit from an Irish Capuchin, who was spiritual director of a seminary. He came simply to meditate with us, having found one of our books in a Dublin bookstore and been taken with the need to communicate the way of meditation to his students who looked to him for their spiritual formation. Each afternoon, behind the thick walls of the old house that kept out the summer heat, we talked of meditation and its contempory importance for the renewal of our religious orders. Out of these discussions much of our next newsletter was derived.

In September an American Benedictine, Father Paul, joined us for six months and began work on a thesis that he would later continue in Paris. The summer still survived and kept us out in the garden or finding odd corners of the exterior that needed paint or repair. The groups that had been suspended for July and August resumed and we were soon back to our former schedule. Many from the groups who could do so joined us during the summer months for our regular community sessions of meditation or the Friday Eucharist and this had reinforced our sense of our primary task—to be there to meditate with whoever came. The summer had given us all the space to relax together and to consider the next step we seemed ready to take.

September 11, 1978

My Dearest Friends,

This letter is quite overdue. But its delay does not betoken any neglect—it is just that since we last wrote, we have had so full a life that it seemed good to postpone writing until we could give you a complete report of how we have developed here in the last few months.

The week of the Abbot's visit was a full and demanding time. But despite the busy program, it was a moving sign for us in the community that he was able to join us each day at our Eucharist and our three sessions of meditation preceded by the

Divine Office. The way this was combined with the round of meetings and engagements symbolized how our own life of prayer itself has led to a deepening openness to all around us. This was a theme taken up by Bishop Crowley when he joined us to preside at our Friday evening Mass. This is part of the Bishop's address to the community on May 26:

> As you all well know, the monastic tradition within the Church has been the source of great riches, spiritually, theologically, artistically, and culturally. Benedict had the great wisdom to recognize that when men or women of singular vision are united in a common life, a common rule, a common purpose, and a common prayer life, great things are possible. The work of the Spirit is greatly facilitated and the life of the Church is immeasurably invigorated. You know better than I the many periods in history when the monastic orders proved to be the mainstay of truly human life and spiritual growth.
>
> However, what we may all be hesitant to recognize, because of the unflagging energy such a recognition demands, is the fact that our own day is calling desperately for a renewal of the monastic spirit and the deepening of the monastic commitment to cultural development. . . .
>
> Without men and women of contemplative vision and spiritual depth, our hopes for building up the kingdom of God's love are destined to be based in the shifting sands of passing fads and momentary movements. What will last must be founded in the vision of the past and must look to the dreams of the future. Only the contemplative spirit of the old and the young together can provide such a pathway for contemporary man.
>
> Benedict also had a clear sense of the early Christian community in the urging to hospitality that he enjoined upon all his brothers and sisters in the following of Christ. This sense of warmth and welcome is so important for all who would come to you seeking the compassion, the understanding, the solicitude of the Good Shepherd. Let this place always be a haven of hope and a citadel of charity for any who come to you—for as has been given to you, so must you give to others. . . .
>
> Quite simply and directly, I invited you to come to Montreal because I know all too well how deeply the clergy, the religious, and the laity of our diocese need a strong center of prayerful hospitality wherein they can drink deep of the timeless values of the Holy Spirit, rendered timely by men of

contemplative vision. I am delighted that you have come; I hope and pray sincerely that you prosper—for your prosperity bespeaks rich and succulent fruit for my priests and people. And, after all, that is what I am here for, too.

The Abbot was the first of many visitors who have made our summer a time of sharing our prayer with others in the way the Bishop described.

A long-term guest was an Irish Capuchin, with us for six weeks, during which we spent an hour or so in conversation each day, and I want to share with you some of the insights that arose in the course of our conversations.

One of the basic insights was to see in a new way the great importance of meditation to the living tradition of the faith. All of us, at least in the West and especially those brought up in Christian homes, receive the tradition as part of our general cultural heritage and as part of the whole system of values and ways of seeing life that we take more or less for granted. The basic Christian values have become so essential a part of our overall cultural formation that it is easy to identify them with a particular type of society and so to lose sight of them as our society and culture evolve. When the Christian tradition loses contact with its own inner dynamic, it not only cannot lead men to build a new society on their experience of these basic values, but it even tends to lose its own self-confidence—the authority that derives from its living contact with its author. The faith tradition we receive on our entry into the Christian community depends for its authenticity and effectiveness on personal experience. It is a tradition of powerful richness and significance and one that is never stale because it is part of a pattern that is still in formation. Each generation, like each individual, has a different past. The perspective of history is in constant change. But all this resourcefulness and dynamism is only potential until it is realized or activated by the personal faith-decision undertaken by each individual as a maturing member of the Christian family. And this decision or commitment of faith is not merely intellectual or dialectical. It is not that we decide to "believe" in the ideas of the Christian tradition. It is much rather that we have the courage and, in a real sense, the recklessness to open ourselves to the unknown, the unfathomable and truly mysterious dimension of the tradition. We allow ourselves, in the full biblical sense, to "know" the mystery or, even better, to be known *by* it. To allow ourselves to do this (a better way of putting it than to say *make* ourselves do it) is to follow the fundamental gospel precept of becoming simple, of becoming childlike, of becoming awake. It is no small cause for wonder that despite the fact that the tradition has been so influential for so long it is so easily forgotten by those in its mainstream that these *are* the fundamental tenets of the gospel of Jesus—that faith is not a matter of exertion but of openness.

We need to see faith in this way as openness, and to see it as a positive, creative, sensitive way of being—miles apart from mere passivity or quietism. The effectiveness of all doing depends on the quality of being we enjoy. And to be open implies certain other qualities: such as being still, because we cannot be open to what is *here* if we are always running after what we think is *there*; such as being silent, because we cannot listen or receive unless we give our whole attention; such as being simple, because what we are being open to is the wholeness, the integrity of God. This condition of openness as the blend of stillness, silence, and simplicity is the condition of prayer; our nature and being in wholesome harmony with the being and nature of God in Jesus.

Meditation is our way to this condition of being fully human, fully alive—a condition we all are called to. To meditate is to stand in the middle—*stare in medio*—and to be conscious that the center is not ourselves but God. And in meditation, therefore, we enter into the living stream of faith that gives meaning to and realizes the tradition that has formed us and which we are responsible for transmitting to those not yet born. We do so by entering the state of faith where we are solely and exclusively open to the personal presence of the living Christ within us, knowing that presence fully and personally, beyond the limitations of language and thought—knowing it "though it is beyond knowledge." This sort of knowledge is of a different order from the sort we acquire and store in studying history, in scientific research, in reading poetry. It is not our objective knowledge of God as an object and could never be because God can never be known as an object—a truth proclaimed by the Christian tradition since Irenaeus, who tells us, "Without God you cannot know God." Only God can know himself and we are called to participate in his knowledge of himself—a calling made feasible because of our union with Jesus. But we have to remind ourselves that this "knowledge" is not a mere intellectualist comprehension of God's greatness, his absoluteness, his compassion. God's self-knowledge is his love, the love that is the Trinity and that is the basic energy and prototype of all creation. God is Love, St. John tells us, and we are called by Love into love.

The immediacy, the urgency of the Christian revelation is that all this is a present reality, established in the center of the human condition, demanding only that we realize it. This is why meditation is neither a backward glance nor a timorous projection forward but rather combines the old and the new in the glory of the eternal present—the "perpetual now." And it is this element in meditation that makes the meditator a truly contemporary person, fully open and alive to the ever-present creative power of God sustaining the universe in being from moment to moment. The liberty to "move with the times," to recognize the changing needs and circumstances of the community or society around us, is the fruit of stability at the center of our being.

It often seems to many people that prayer is an introspective state and that the meditator is someone going into himself to the exclusion of the people and creation around him, that he is socially irrelevant. Nothing could be further from the truth. As the Bishop said in his talk, not only is the timeless contemplative vision the necessary basis for contemporary action but it is the essential condition for a fully human response to life—to the richness, the unpredictability, the sheerly *given* quality of life. The persistent temptation of which we have to be constantly alert is that we opt for the half-life that denies the present reality of the Incarnation: either seeking all value in the world or all in spirit. Because of Christ alive and active in the human heart and man's social relationships, the two are gloriously interfused, and so a monk of such deep wakefulness as Abhishiktananda could write these words:

> The soul tastes the supreme joy of being not only in the cave of the heart, but also in the endless multiplicity of her contacts with the world of men and nature of which she is part. Every moment is a sacrament of eternity; every event a sign and sacrament of the perfect Bliss; for nothing in the universe can escape being transformed by the divine *Eschaton* — and by its sign in the Eucharist — at every moment of time.
> (*Saccidananda* — ISPCK Delhi, 1974, p. 186)

Abhishiktananda describes how the inmost center of man's soul opens up from within, in the power of Christ's love dwelling there, and opens toward the reality in which it knows itself forever a part — neither "inward" nor "outward" but simply "with." It is by entering this essential experience of our faith that modern men and women will be able to avoid the real danger of a modernistic gnosis — of attempting to reduce God and his infinity within the limitations of our finite minds. This is the hubris against which theology must be guarded. Meditation is so important because it leads us beyond the images and concepts that we can so easily use to try to control the divine presence. It leads us indeed beyond all egotistic "desire" for God. At the other end of the scale is the danger for the modern religious mind of a new sort of quietism — a new sort of passive sentimentality. Prayer, above all else, is not a nostalgia for God. Prayer is the summons to a full experience of the living Christ whose purpose, as St. Paul tells us, "is everywhere at work." St. Paul's emphasis is not on religion as anesthesia — thinking about the absent God and absenting ourselves from the present moment to be lost in a kind of pietistic dalliance. For Paul, the summons of the authentic religious intuition in humankind is to enter fully and courageously into the present moment, there to be filled with life by the living Christ. The call of prayer, in short, is to be fully alive in the present, without regret for the past or fear of the future.

And so we have to accept the responsibility of being alive — of understanding the full significance and depth of mystery contained in the Christian experience. This experience—in essence the experience of being fully open to our own humanity and gift of our creation—is nothing less than conscious participation in the self-knowledge of God. This is the direct message of St. Paul:

> For the same God who said,"Out of darkness let light shine" has caused his light to shine within us, to give the light of revelation, the revelation of the glory of God in the face of Jesus. (2 Cor. 4:6)

What is clear is that for us, God is never an object that we know—the truth is so much greater than this. Our own potential for wholeness is precisely that he knows us and in that complete knowledge we know. We have always to remember, too, that we know him not just speculatively in our minds but existentially in our hearts, in the fullness and richness of a prayer that leaves self entirely behind and plunges into the depths of God himself with no thought for self but entirely "living for him who for our sake died and was raised to life" (2 Cor. 5:16).

We keep you in our hearts and send you all much love.

Every blessing,

John Main, OSB

Letter Five (DECEMBER 1978)

As we approached the first anniversary of our arrival, the community continued to grow in size and, because of new and gifted lay members, in variety. We were also more and more in contact with French-speaking Quebecers who heard of us and came to meditate with us or learn of what we were doing. The French-speaking Church here had undergone a traumatic reversal of fortune in the past fifteen years and the massive decline in religious practice had created a spiritual vacuum that many movements had come to fill. Many who now came to us had begun meditating as a result of an encounter with TM but were looking again at their own tradition from the new standpoint that their experience of the inner journey had won for them. Almost all were amazed to hear of a contemplative tradition in Christianity that was addressed to all and was not the privilege of a spiritual elite. "Why have we never heard about this before?" they would ask. How, indeed, could the Gospels and St. Paul be read daily in churches and yet the experience of prayer they convey be so unknown to the bulk of Christians?

A small group of artists and craftsmen began to work on a number of projects in our basement, although we still lacked the space and facilities to develop proper opportunities for manual work for members of the community or guests. We knew this was important for giving a personal balance to our lives, both from our experience so far and from the essential Benedictine principle of the synthesis among prayer, work, and study. It was another indication that the development of our work required more space.

St. Benedict said a monastery will never be without guests and we were a proof of it. He said also the monks must pray with the guests and this was why our guests came. We suggested that newcomers join us in meditation for two sessions each day, morning and evening, and when it seemed natural to do so, to come to the midday session also. It was important, especially with all living at close quarters, to avoid any sense of constraint or obligation because the journey can only be undertaken in perfect liberty and followed with a self-renewing commitment. It was clear that the witness to this was the most important teaching we had to offer and it was made as a community who had learned it from their own experience. Every member of the community shared this witness and it was underpinned by the absolute and permanent commitment of the monastic life.

In the fall we published a new set of tapes and booklet, "The Christian Mysteries: Prayer and Sacrament," which had grown out of talks I had given to a meeting of priests of the diocese. In this we tried to put meditation before the more liturgically oriented Christian by stressing the essential need for a personal journey of prayer if the outward celebrations were to be really signs and moments of growth in spiritual maturity. It had been clear more than once that our first three tapes on meditation often made deeper contact with the Christian or the non-Christian to whom "religion" or "worship" were secondary or unfamiliar. In Ireland these tapes had proved very popular with groups of Alcoholics Anonymous.

We made the next important step in the community's development in October when we visited Mount Saviour. Albert Reyburn, their devoted Oblate, Father Paul, Brother Laurence, and I drove down through New York State's beautiful fall colors and we were greeted very warmly by the Prior, Father Martin Boler. He listened with interest to our account of the Montreal foundation and of the crossroads we had reached in our monastic development. He and the community offered us their support and patronage for any step we would take to respond to the new opportunity then shaping itself before us.

December 6, 1978

My Dearest Friends,

Greetings in the Lord! Firstly, on behalf of everyone here let me wish you all a most happy and joyful celebration of the Lord's birth.

We are very conscious of what it means to celebrate an anniversary as it was exactly a year ago today that we moved into this house. It is with a sense of wonder and gratitude that we look back over the last year to see how we have begun our work as a monastery in the city, grateful for the new members who have joined the community as well as hopeful for the future that opens up ahead of us.

As we have all seen the Community here grow and develop during the last year, it has reminded us of the generosity of spirit that still makes the Rule of St. Benedict an inspiration of the monastic life fourteen hundred years after it was written. Although Benedict wrote for a particular time and for a particular type of monk, his own experience of the liberty of spirit that the gospel proclaims enabled him to avoid writing a rigid rule book. His vision and perspective are powerfully highlighted not only because he sees the Rule as applying only to a phase of the monastic vocation — "a little rule for beginners" — but also, and most importantly for his modern disciples, when he allows for the use of discretion in living the Rule in different contexts. He saw that the details and so the form of the monastic life would be conditioned by the place and people that shape it. And it is precisely because of this insertion into its own time and place that a monastery has relevance in its social and cultural context. Because it is relevant it can relate to its contemporaries in contemporary terms, and because it can relate it can also serve. It serves by showing the society into which it is inserted that the ultimate meaning of men and women is found beyond themselves, beyond their culture and tradition. It does not do this by naively denouncing the secular — monks have passed through the same formative experiences in society as everyone else. It testifies by the way it arranges its priorities of living to show that the end of all our searching is only found by the way of transcendence. But its great Christian proclamation is that the seeds of the transcendent experience are planted in the soil of our humanity and our culture. Our spiritual journey does not call for a rupture with our humanity but the fulfillment of it, the natural continuation of it.

The experience of transcendence is not, therefore, one that we can engineer or fit into our own timetable of relative priorities: first, because it is pure gift, and second, because by its nature it involves our whole person and there is no curious reflecting ego left to stand outside the experience as detached observer. The experience occurs within the nature of things — our nature — the parables of the Kingdom show that the essence of this experience is natural growth. A small mustard seed grows into a tree big enough for the birds to come and roost in its branches (Matt. 13:31-33). To try to make it grow faster or slower would be absurd and counterproductive. It is the same when we experience the growth of the Kingdom in our hearts as we follow the journey of meditation. Day by day we let the husk of the ego drop away and like a seed we die to self that we may fulfill the destiny that is our true meaning, that the potential of life within us may come to full fruition. It is the same, too, when a monastic community or, indeed, any Christian community takes root and allows the love of God to fill and expand it. The Christian vision has always respected the processes of natural growth—grace building on nature—because it has always seen that our redemption means precisely that all human growth is now incorporate in Christ and shares the limitless achievement he has won. The mystery of the fully mature Christ is *infinite* growth. The mystery, as St. Paul wrote, is Christ within you.

The natural process of the Christian experience explains why Christianity is both transcendent and incarnational. And this is why a Christian community realizes and manifests an experience of transcendence while it is at the same time fully, naturally human. Indeed, *because* it is human, a Christian community is not concerned with an ideal but with a reality. In its full revelation we know this reality—which is the reality of love—as divine, as the mystery of the Being of God. But we begin to experience it in its human revelation first, by the love we have for others and the love they show us. There is nothing abstract or generalized about this. It means realizing that *this* brother or *this* sister is a temple of the love of God and that he or she must be loved and reverenced both for this mystery of creation as well as for his or her frailty of temperament or faith. In realizing this, we know the mystery of what it is to be a person—unique and of infinite importance in the love of God.

Perhaps the greatest social service a monastery can contribute is to be a place where this fundamental truth of human life—the truth upon which any sane society must rest—can be experienced in its purity and directness. To know that each of us has an infinite importance and value is the first step. The second, and greater, is to know that this empowers us to turn away from self to another in love. Indeed, a monastery reveals that these two steps are actually one reality. We find ourselves by loving: finding ourselves means knowing ourselves to be loved. St. Benedict puts this very vividly:

> This zeal, therefore, monks should practice with the most burning love so as to be the first in showing honor to each other. Let them bear with weaknesses whether of body or of character with the most tolerant patience. Let them vie with one another in showing mutual obedience. Let no one follow what he thinks is useful to himself but what is of use to another. (Chapter 72)

Medieval monastic writers were fond of emphasizing that the monastic life in Benedict's vision was essentially the Christian life "writ large." And indeed it is not only the monastic community today that is called to be a beacon of love in the Church or in the world. But the monastery is special because it is an enduring, available sign of the practicality and possibility of this life. A person may be encouraged and inspired by reading the gospels. He is doubly so by seeing the gospel lived in single-minded generosity of spirit. A monastery can make this witness in many different ways but it will always do so less by theory than by practice. Its particular call is not to talk about the Christian experience as much as to live it, to communicate it, to *be* it.

Visitors to the monastery often come with unclear motives. They may not know where or how to begin a journey whose call they can nevertheless neither evade nor shake off. So what they first experience often surprises them. They think they will find God in the terms they have imagined until then. But instead they first find themselves—recognized, known, and inexplicably loved. And because of that experience their expectations begin to change. They no longer seek a God of their own imagining. Instead, they begin to expand in the presence of the God they know to be beyond thought or image. They begin to realize that their seeking often served merely to lock them blindly into themselves and to tie them to the limitations of images. Far more wonderful, they now realize that God is seeking them. They must simply be still and allow themselves to be found. All this is, of course, something only experience can teach, and a loving community can provide the context for the discovery. The monk is one who follows through this discovery in such a context. He is one who, by his own commitment to the journey, is called to help create and strengthen the community where others, maybe by a brief contact with it, can find their way.

Every Christian knows at some level of his or her being that the central mystery of faith is the experience of love. We know it and yet such is the timidity and inconstancy of our hearts that we need to hear the Word spoken anew day by day; and we do hear it in the word spoken to us by our brethren as well as in the silence of our meditation. We hear it spoken in the community, which is the locus, the context where the Word of God is in ceaseless utterance. The silence that must be so integral a part of a monastic community serves just this end—that we may always hear the reverberations of the Word and know its utterance as the mystery of Christ's presence among us. To hear it just once is to be reassured and fortified in the depth of our being. To hear it always is to live a life impregnated with a "joy too great for words" (1 Peter 1:9) and to realize ever more fully that we are "incorporate with Christ." So profound is this incorporation that we have shared his death and rising—we are his. And we are bidden to enter just as profound a union with one another. Paul called his communities "brethren in the Lord" and our brother is our brother precisely because of what Jesus has achieved for both of us.

Bonhoeffer wrote, "God hates visionary dreaming." The monastic community is one where the truth is being lived, not just stated—the truth that the gospel is not about ideals but reality, not about delay but beginning. As the Rule of St. Benedict shows, this means that a Christian community consists in loving people as they are. "The man who fashions a visionary ideal of community, Bonhoeffer went on to say, "demands that it be realized by God, by others, by himself. . . . He acts as if he is the creator of Christian community—as if his dream binds men together." And when this egotistic ideal is destroyed, the dreamer accuses his brethren, his God, and, finally, in despair, himself.

This goes to show what we were saying at the beginning of this letter. The process of Christian growth, whether for individual or for community, is natural. And its ultimate meaning is always a mystery. The real contribution of a monastic community to secular society is far more profound than it may seem on the surface. The great practical touchstone of a monastic community is its seriousness. Its seriousness keeps it developing in harmony with the mystery that contains its secret meaning. And to be serious is the opposite of being solemn. To be serious is to accept the fact that we are created for ultimate happiness, that being and joy are coexistent. A monastery is a place of joy—capable, too, of having fun without being distracted from its purpose. It is a joy that permeates every aspect of the community. I notice it sometimes in the way we enter the meditation room together, in the way we experience each other's joy in painting a wall, making a picture, publishing an article, or creating a successful Boeuf Bourgignonne. In such ways a loving community can communicate a unique experience of the unity of our lives—that I am not many people living different lives but one person involved in the mystery of communion with my own destiny, with others, with God. The condition for this experience is a joy-filled seriousness and this is the fruit of simplicity and commitment. The monastic life is not set over against the ordinary Christian life but it is simply a special arrangement of priorities that can constitute the Christian life anywhere. It is this arrangement that the monk understands, freely chooses, and generously undertakes (Chapter 58 of the Rule). These priorities are not rules to be imposed but form a life-style growing out of a shared vision that is authenticated both by the tradition and by our personal experience.

Because of this seriousness lived in an expansive, hospitable spirit of love, the monastery fulfills a prophetic role. It points to the ultimate sadness of a life built on mere fun-seeking; to the destructiveness of distraction; to the insecurity and isolation created by triviality. It does not expose all this merely by denouncing it; it incarnates a positive, experienced alternative of fullness of life. It shows that this is a possibility. No one would deny that at this point in the twentieth century monasticism has serious thinking to do about its future. What is becoming clearer every year is that a modern monasticism is more aware than ever of its primitive origins and basic impulse. It knows of the centrality of meditation in the tradition of monastic prayer, the universal relevance of the values it proclaims by being fully human, fully loving. More and more it will fulfill its prophetic role by living in the cities where the experience of community and of spirit are all but lost. There, in these modern deserts, it will bloom by the proof of the power of faith and absolute generosity to achieve the impossible in liberty of spirit. "Let the wilderness and thirsty land be glad; Let the desert rejoice and burst into flower" (Isa. 35:1). The proof of the liberty, the flexibility of spirit that is the essence of monasticism, is the spectrum of the monastic life. Some communities will pray in the city and lead people onto the way. Others will witness far from the city in a life more explicitly rooted in the cycle of nature. Still others will meet what is the very special contemporary challenge of reconciling these two dimensions within the same community experience—service and solitude, city and village, cloister and marketplace.

The link between these two dimensions is anyway unbreakable. To try to break it is to pursue a dream, to create a self-centered rather than the other-centered community, which alone is loving. So let me stress again that what we are talking about is not an abstract, ideal world, but the world as it is: the fallen world but the world redeemed, the world of sin and heroism, suffering and joy, madness and sanity, pain and comforting, all redeemed by love. This is the self-contradictory world in which we gain our experience of community, and the power of this experience is that it transforms self-contradiction into paradox. The paradox is then the way of transcendence.

The communion Christians share is not an ideal we have to create but the reality created by God in Christ in whom we have our being and meaning. It is a communion that reveals greater and greater depths, deeper and deeper centers. The more we can understand this, the more serene and the more liberating will be our experience of community.

Thankfulness is an essential part of this experience—thankful to God for the Word he has given us, to the community for the opportunities it offers. Real thankfulness for this experience is the basis of all meaningful celebration. But it is a sadly rare phenomenon in a world geared to acquisition rather than thanksgiving. So it is not just a platitude to say how deeply thankful we are for that community we know we share with all of you on the same daily pilgrimage. For the sake of discussion we talk of different levels and kinds of growth but we know that the mystery is that there is only one process of growth, which we all share in. That is the building up in love of the one body of Christ—the body of which we are the parts. "Let us speak the truth in love; so shall we fully grow up into Christ" (Eph. 4:15).

To know that this transcendent mystery is humanly rooted in our daily lives and our loving relationships with each other is the great source of Christian joy—and the great power of the Christian presence in the world. What St. Benedict says of monks in the last chapter of the Rule expresses the generosity of the universal Christian family that finds its unity and vitality in the presence of Jesus: "Let them put absolutely nothing before Christ and may he bring us all together to life eternal."

We keep you all in our hearts every day. We send you a message of joy to persevere in the growth of the Lord Jesus in our hearts and throughout the world.

With much love,

John Main, OSB

Letter Six (MARCH 1979)

O ur second Christmas in Montreal helped us to realize how deeply we had put down our roots here. The gestures of friendship we received and the amount of outside participation in our liturgies and meditation were all signs of the adaptation we had barely felt taking place. Yet, just after Christmas, visits from members of the English groups reminded us of a real continuity between our work and life there and here. How fertile this mutual influence could be was made evident in early January when a group from North Carolina drove up to see us to discuss models of community living for a number of families who had been meeting together for prayer and were now looking for a deeper commitment to the journey they were on. One of the leaders of a London meditation group and Bishop Crowley of Montreal were able to discuss with them and us how such a scheme could be made viable. It was an opportunity, too, to air some of the ideas we had been putting together in the form of a "Rule" for communities based on a common commitment to meditation — a rule that aimed not to describe structures of life as much as to clarify the principles and some of the practical considerations of a modern contemplative community. Many of the experiments we heard of in this line seemed to fail precisely because there was no inner coherence, no unifying *doctrina*. This could, of course, be due to a basic lack of commitment. But the inevitable difficulties could also be compounded by the lack of clear language. One of the problems we talked about was how to find a precise vocabulary to replace our largely devalued religious language. How were we to communicate the meaning of "discipline," "obedience," or "faith" without which there could no human community, contemplative or otherwise?

At the end of January I left for England to fulfill some long-standing engagements and retreats. Brother Laurence took on the responsibility for the groups and general care of the community.

I spent the first week at Ealing, where the community was about to receive new novices and where I had the opportunity to talk to everyone together about the way our foundation had developed. While in London I also spoke to several of the meditation groups that had been formed from our Center. I visited the Fellowship of St. Ethelwold in Abingdon and spent a weekend with people from meditation groups around England at the Grail's center in Pinner.

I went by train to Scotland where I gave the annual retreat to the Trappists' community at Nunraw. From there to Ireland and a week's retreat to some longtime friends, the Medical Missionaries of Mary in Drogheda, an order with houses in Africa, Europe and the Americas. The transition from one place to another, from the lay men and women in the groups and the Grail to the contemplative Trappists, was instructive at every level. It showed me the essential continuity of the search for God among people, regardless of their condition of life. And the universal question was always, "But how?" It seemed to me that the generalities with which people had been conditioned no longer satisfied them. The search for God, for absolute value and personal meaning, was a search for a way to pray, to find God in self and self in God and, above all, to find a way that was possible for modern men and women.

I was brought closer still to this search by some days spent in Dublin, where an old friend, Father Tom Fehily, a parish priest, had organized a series of meetings. After a day with a group of Capuchins brought together by the Irish Capuchin who had been with us in Montreal the previous summer, I went to Father Tom, met one of his meditation groups and a class in his parish school, gave a talk at University College and another to a large meeting at Mount Sackville. My last engagement in Ireland was with the Kiltegan Fathers in County Wicklow, whose superior had spent time with us in Montreal on his return from Africa. At their house I was able to meet, after a long period of correspondence, Bishop Moynagh, who had spent many years in service of the Nigerian Church.

The long round of meetings of the previous weeks had encouraged me in what we were trying to do in Montreal by giving our work there a wider perspective. The problems, the opportunieis, the search were essentially the same everywhere and the attempt to confront them in any one place was not isolated from other attempts or the experience of other places. The message our life was trying to express in Montreal was to speak to people in their deepest concern for spirit and truth—and the message is the Word spoken in silence. To hear this same message communicated in other places and in diverse ways can only encourage one's own efforts and further expand one's own vision. I have found that the only ultimately tiring exercise is talking about meditation to people who want only to talk about it with no intention of practicing it. Nearly everywhere I had spoken I had been with people who were on the pilgrimage or were seriously trying to begin it. When I returned to Montreal my tiredness was only physical and I could look to the future with new energy.

March 21, 1979
Feast of Saint Benedict

My Dearest Friends,

Peace and love in the Lord.

It seems a long time since we have written to you, but as I had the joy of seeing so many of you while I was in England, Ireland, and Scotland, I hope you will forgive our long silence. So much has happened since December when we sent you the last newsletter.

Before Christmas Bishop Crowley came and presided at our evening liturgy. In his homily he said, "The tremendous grace that this community can offer to an alienated, exiled world can indeed bring men back to the Spirit where they will find happiness to be like a river. . . . But first we must respond deeply within our hearts to the Lord our God who teaches all goodness."

We have indeed become more clearly conscious that the service that a community of prayer fulfills within a society must be an integrated response to the deepest needs and yearnings of man. The monastery in the world is like a sacrament of the monastic dimension in every man and woman; and the pilgrimage of prayer, followed within a fraternity of love that *is* the monastic communion, is the same journey from the illusion of the ego to the reality of God that every person is called to make. There is no way any society can achieve internal harmony or belief in its own meaning without such centers of spiritual simplicity and commitment operating in peace and seriousness out of resources that are beyond social control. The call of God that draws us to himself both transcends and justifies society because it is always a call of love that demands a response of love, which, although rooted in the ordinary fabric of our lives, travels into the infinite space of God where call and response are consummated in the eternal moment of Being.

Our daily lives can often seem so routine and uninspiring that the perspective of this vision of life is lost or becomes merely a memory we carry around with us from books we have read or retreats we have attended. But, of course, reality cannot be either remembered or imagined: it can only be experienced in the utter liberty of the present moment, which underlies and pervades all our activity and growth. If it seems that this moment comes and goes it is indeed only seeming. The experience was not absent. We were absent. And the illusion of its absence, like all illusion, was caused by our consciousness being centered in ourselves rather than in the Other—self-referring rather than God-referring. In all our prayer here we keep you in our hearts so that you will keep on this joyful pilgrimage, always more deeply entering yourselves in the loving Otherness of God with every greater courage. Many of you will know that it takes a certain spirit of recklessness to set out on the journey from self. We may not be happy with our self-centeredness but at least its unhappiness is predictable, while the unknown that lies outside the circle of our desiring and sadness constantly defeats our powers of anticipation and, more and more literally, has to be taken on faith. Many of you will know, too, the moments of anger, grief, or absurdity that occur as it becomes more obvious that our way to knowledge is the way of unknowing. But they are only moments on the straight path to the single Moment. And because the power by which we follow this path is not our own, these moments hold no ultimate sway over us. In going through them the recklessness with which we started the journey is steadily transformed into an ever deepening generosity by the discipline of our daily meditation.

It was a joyful thing to see this realized in so many of the groups I met with—groups that were not complicating or saddening the journey with unnecessary effort of self-centeredness but persevering in simplicity of heart and in openness to the Lord living in their hearts. The people in these groups were setting their minds upon the kingdom as their first priority, ever more generous communicants of the perfecting power of faith, which is our openness to the reality beyond us, yet containing us.

While enjoying the kindness and hospitality of the missionaries in Drogheda, I also had the opportunity to visit and talk with some Dominican sisters. On a very cold winter's afternoon we talked together of the love of God known in prayer and experienced in our own hearts and then marvelously communicated and shared with all we meet. As we sat in the common room before a turf fire, whose soft light grew stronger and more beautiful as the evening wore on, it was natural to see in that moment a sign of what we were sharing at a deeper level of reality. The power of human love is the fire of God's love centered in each person and each community of persons and realized when each of us turns toward this center and allows its light to illumine us.

Finding the same openhearted seeking among groups that had come together in such different ways in England, Scotland, and Ireland also highlighted the dynamic of community formation that always accompanies the search for God. The journey into the God who is Love cannot be followed in isolation — we cannot determine the itinerary of our own pilgrimage or the conditions of our own commitment. Indeed, when we find ourselves "planning" our own inner journey, steering our course so as to catch the sights on the way, it is a sure sign that we have yet to take our hand off the wheel so as to let the God-motivated direction reveal itself — we have not, to put it another way, placed our center of consciousness outside of ourselves. The community is the context in which we learn the truth and power of other-centeredness. And our fidelity to the community — our loving openness and freedom with others — is, as it were, the complement to our fidelity to the mantra — our generous and magnanimous poverty of spirit. The way of meditation is only the way of love: "this work of love," as *The Cloud of Unknowing* calls it. And so it is real, not theoretical; incarnate, not abstract; practical, not just a matter of words or ideas. To act upon this vision and really to begin the journey requires a decisive and open commitment. There is, though, no commitment without the simplicity of spirit that allows us to say an unambiguous "yes" to the invitation to journey to reality. The danger of this, of course, is that it sounds like — and can lead us into — the worst form of self-centered self-importance . . . until we understand that the "yes" we utter is Christ himself.

> The Son of God, Christ Jesus, proclaimed among you by
> us . . . was never a blend of Yes and No. With him it was and is
> Yes. He is the Yes pronounced upon God's promises, every
> one of them. That is why, when we give glory to God, it is
> through Christ Jesus that we say "Amen." (1 Cor. 1:19-21)

Our commitment is already pledged in the transcendent power
of Jesus, the proof of which is his Spirit dwelling in our hearts. It
remains for us to realize through our own simplicity that the
incorporation in his achievement is pure gift. And so our way is
the way of simplicity: the simplicity of our word and the
simplicity of love.

What is so clear is that the time in which we live is a moment
in history when men and women everywhere in every tradition
and culture are recognizing that the journey within is the
journey absolutely necessary if our evolution is to continue.
Everywhere people are trying to open their eyes, yearning for
that gift and expansion of consciousness that is the vision of God
within and beyond each one of us. The central task of the
Church is to respond to that basic intuition in humankind and to
lead us to the knowledge that our eyes are opened if we would
only see with the mind of Christ. This is a matter of knowledge,
not talk. And it is the task of all serious Christians to confirm
people in their search by leading them into the richness and
depth of their own lived experience.

The serious commitment to prayer of the Medical
Missionaries of Mary, for example, finds compassionate
expression in their great work of healing throughout the world.
Mother Mary Martin, their foundress, remains an effective and
mature inspiration to them because she was so evidently a
woman of deep prayer, deep faith, and deep compassion. She
saw clearly and knew out of her own experience that the
grounding reality of the Christian life is our experience of
prayer and that when this is entered into with generosity and
commitment, we enter, both personally and communally, into
the place assigned to us in the harmony of the love of God at
work in the world: the harmony that is the Body of Christ.

To end, I would like to try to put before you the core of
what I attempted to say to so many of the groups on this journey.

What brought the experience of those weeks into a unity was not so much what was said or discussed as the silence of meditation shared at each place with each person. But this silence and openness to the mystery of our being together in his name at that time and place, to the mystery of his presence within and among us, would have been impossible without fundamental simplicity of heart. To tread the way of meditation requires only simplicity of heart. Our talking, our thinking and reading, and our theology have value, but only to the degree that they lead us to this disposition of openness and continue to deepen our childlikeness. St. John of the Cross put this very clearly in Book 1 of *The Ascent of Mount Carmel*:

> Only those who set aside their own knowledge and walk in God's service like unlearned children receive wisdom from God. . . ."If any one among you thinks he is wise let him become ignorant so as to be wise. For the wisdom of this world is foolishness with God" (1 Cor. 3:18-19). Accordingly, a man must advance in union with God's wisdom by unknowing rather than by knowing. (4:5)

The cloud of this unknowing is the cloud by which the presence of God as well as the inner nature of his hiddenness is so often described in the Bible. A cloud that both leads us through the desert (Exod. 13:22) and draws us into itself to speak the Word (Luke 9:35) —the cloud, too, in which we have only to say our little word (*The Cloud of Unknowing*, Chap. 7).

In our prayer we set aside our own knowledge together with our expectations and our memories in order that we may be wholly open to the Word of God in the present moment and in purity of heart. And we have the courage to do this because we believe with our whole heart at a level beyond desire, sorrow, or imagination that God's Word is alive, active, and in continual utterance. This is faith beyond what we normally call belief, a faith that is at once courage, commitment, and openness. And through it we come to know that the reality of God is the source and power of our own reality, to know it "though it is beyond knowledge." Our pilgrimage is only to the simplicity that is the condition of entering faithfully and courageously into the silence of selflessness where we awake to hear this utterance and to attend to it with our whole beings. The wonder of prayer is that we hear this Word addressed to us directly and personally, without the distracting obfuscation of our own "wisdom." In hearing this we learn that we are continuously being called into being by Being. We therefore share in the eternal presentness of God, the God who calls himself "I AM." Because prayer is not our prayer: it is his. The mystery, beyond words, is that we are invited to be fully open to it with the power of his own love.

What all of us have to learn—lay men and women, monks, students, children, sisters, housewives, and priests—is that the purpose of all theology and worship, and of life itself, is simply to awaken us to the supreme reality that God IS and that his Spirit lives in our hearts. This is the journey that the New Testament calls the way of faith—a way that begins and ends in faith. It is a journey away from familiar limitations and illusions into an unknown space where we find ourselves in reality. There we are summoned to full wakefulness and full being. It is not that we awaken to reality as if it were something external and objectifiable or as if it could be remembered. Rather, we awaken in reality—in which we live and move and have our being.

Our life of prayer is something essential for us. It is therefore an entirely natural part of our life and what we were created for. Modern life has encapsulated us in so many illusions that keep us always at one remove from reality that we have to take a decisive step into the freedom that bursts all bonds. And that is why our dedication to the times of our meditation every morning and every evening is so fundamental. That is why, too, the faithful recitation of our mantra in those times of the work is of such power.

I spent the weeks in Europe talking about the Spirit and the power of the Spirit working in our hearts and our communities. What I tried to make crystal clear and wholly conscious to all the different groups was that all the talk in the world about prayer and the Spirit is of no avail unless we take the steps necessary to enter into the experience of the Spirit. That entrance is pure gift and in order to enter into the gift we are called to purity of heart and poverty of spirit—the purpose and condition of our meditation.

We hope to be able to send you a letter soon again in the Easter season when the great symbols of the Resurrection still have their springtime power and beauty. In the meantime, we ask you all to keep us here in your hearts. The Community is at a sensitive moment of growth when we hope to expand, to receive new members, and extend our work. As the Easter liturgies will soon be teaching us, the power of all new life comes from beyond ourselves, yet its source has been planted in our inmost being. The journey we share is to this source.

With much love,

John Main, OSB

Letter Seven (JUNE 1979)

B y the following June we had transferred our monastic stability and association from Ealing to Mount Saviour.

In our newsletter of that June we expressed our gratitude to everyone whose generosity had made this transition possible. We knew that not all foundations have found their canonical status as amicably and smoothly as we had done. We were now awaiting three things—the authorization from Rome for starting our own novitiate, the discovery of a suitable site in the Montreal area, and new monastic candidates.

The lay community could provide a form of participation in our life that would allow anyone thinking of joining us as a monk to test and clarify his vocation. This was not its only or even main purpose, of course, nor would it be the most suitable postulancy for all monastic candidates. But it was our hope to avoid too much structural rigidity in both monastic and lay areas of our life while accepting clearly the distinction between temporary and permanent commitment. There were several people who questioned whether this could be possible in the common, personal commitment to pray together. Within that common commitment to daily meditation together, so many of the secondary issues that can torment communities in endless discussions find their natural and obvious resolution.

Our guests always increased in numbers as summer approached and we again had the familiar problem of lack of space. Their variety of age and background continued to enrich our life—from the Anglican Bishop of Ontario to workers from L'Arche and students from the States. Benedictines and other religious were also appearing more frequently. The monks of St. Peter's Abbey in Saskatchewan joined several of our Montreal acquaintances in helping to build up our library. And the text of the first three tapes on meditation appeared in book form to give a further expression of the fundamental commitment we were laying in these early days. Many of the groups and individuals using the tapes as aids to their own journey of meditation had asked us to issue the text of the tapes to deepen the quality of their listening to them. We had always felt the spoken word was the primary medium for communicating the message of meditation but if, as many were confident, the printed word would enhance the power of the spoken, we were happy to put the book in their hands.

In March and April I gave a series of talks at the Faculty of Religious Studies at McGill University. The idea for the course originated with a group of theology students who, like their counterparts in many theological schools, felt the lack of a common living experience of the faith they were spending so many pressured hours in studying. In these meetings, therefore, we tried to integrate our experience of faith in the shared silence of meditation that is the "knowledge" that transcends knowing and integrates the whole person in mind and heart. The students were open and responsive, both in the talk that preceded the meditation and the discussion after it—the same receptivity I had found at the University College in Dublin and with students in California. It seemed there was a certain value in putting the message over in the language of the colleges and schools. But more and more it proved the need for a place that was committed to the experience-in-itself rather than to any of the countless ways it can be expressed—a place that St. Benedict called a "School of the Lord's service"—the monastery, which, by being peripheral to the institutions of learning and administration, testifies to the centrality of the experience of God.

June 24, 1979
Feast of St. John the Baptist

My Dearest Friends,

Greetings in the Lord. So much has happened since we last wrote to you on St. Benedict's day in March. We must apologize for the delay in sending you this letter, but although we have been out of sight during these months, all of you have been in our prayers, in our hearts.

The first news we have to give you is that after consultation with the Abbot of Ealing, it seemed best for us to join with a monastery that was more oriented to the contemplative vision of monasticism. And so we are now a Dependent Priory of Mount Saviour and we hope soon to establish our own novitiate here with the right to profess monks for this House.

Every Benedictine House always has its own special character and direction. As each House pursues its own vision of the monastic journey, it deepens its rediscovery of the tradition that has led it to where it is. In fact, the vision itself is the result of the meeting of tradition with the unique circumstances of the present—a meeting that takes place in the openheartedness of faith. The monastery's responsibility is to integrate its vision with the tradition and to do what it is called to do in passing on the monastic experience of faith to the future. It must, therefore, be able to train its members in the light of its own vision. Our own call has been to follow the path of prayer. We hope to be faithful to that call and to share our contemplative understanding of monasticism both with those who join us as monks and those who live with us for short or long periods—indeed, with all who follow the Way.

Mount Saviour, founded by Father Damasus Winzen in the 1950s, is rooted in this contemplative tradition and we consider it a privilege to have been received into their family and allowed to share their heritage. Another monastery is also attached to Mount Saviour—Christ in the Desert Monastery, also a Dependent Priory, in New Mexico. Our three Houses therefore represent the expanse of the contemplative life through different traditions and in different settings—country, city, and desert. But this, it seems to us, points up the essential unity of the life, its freedom from constriction by outward form, its adaptability to circumstance, its fidelity to the stillness of Being, beyond all complexity and division.

We hope to open our novitiate here in September and we are looking for a larger site to begin the development of the monastery. We hope, too, that that Lord of the harvest will send workers into his vineyard who will generously seek his kingdom, opening their hearts to him in pure consciousness.

Our many guests and visitors in recent weeks have again shown that a community that meditates together and regularly shares the Eucharist and Office finds itself sharing itself at all other sorts of levels of life and being. This is as natural as the bursting of a tree into leaf or the blooming of a flower—the great natural growth symbols of the parables of the Kingdom. The marvelous thing is that this happens again and again and each time as a new miracle, a fresh act of creation filling us with more wonder. This is so, I think, because a community corporately devoted to prayer is bringing to birth its own wholeness. This wholeness—its holiness—literally fills us with wonder because we come to know more and more deeply its potential for infinite expansion. There is no limit to goodness. The experience of Being is, simply and in itself, pure joy, pure thanksgiving. The silence of meditation opens us to this as a present reality. The theoretical and abstract give way to the real and concrete dimension of Eucharist. In that dimension we begin to see the presence of a light shining in and through all things, all our experience, bringing ourselves and our lives into unity. As this light grows stronger and as we are able to perceive and feel it more clearly, we become filled with that joy and peace the New Testament proclaims and communicates—the joy of the Spirit, the peace that passes all understanding.

There is such widespread misunderstanding about the "contemplative life"—the very phrase carries with it so many unconscious associations. To many it summons up a picture of lifeless people sitting around all day with little or nothing to do. But real prayer, coming from the silent center of our spirit, is the source of the selflessness of love, the source of energy. In that center, the source of our Being, we encounter God in the power of his own self-awareness that is his Spirit, the Spirit of Jesus freely "lavished upon us." To find God is to find love. To find love is to find oneself in harmony with the basic energy of all creation, which is love. When a community is directed to this as its essential priority, ordinary limitations imposed on human relations by egoism become, as it were, flipped around. Where there was self-seeking there becomes service. Where there was desire for self-perfection there becomes an impulse to lead others to fulfillment through love. The loving service of a spiritual community derives its stream of inspiration from sharing its openness to the One who became the servant of us all.

In our retreats and guests you can see something of our development on the monastic journey with our hopes for a novitiate and future monks praying, working, studying, and proclaiming the Kingdom by the simplicity of their lives and the joy of their spirits. And the fact that this can mean so much to those who are not monks shows that there is a common experience that links the monastery to other forms of life in the Spirit. Merton spoke in his later years of the monastic dimension in every person. This is the dimension of faith. I would like to end this letter by saying something about faith, because it is faith, coming from a deep and living spring in us, that makes the monastic adventure not only a possibility but such a rich and joyful experience for those who can embrace it with generosity.

We use the single word "faith" to cover a vast range of human experience. For St. Paul, the whole Christian life was shaped by faith: the Way began in faith and ended in faith. This totality of faith suggests how fundamental it is to the life of our spirit. Faith is, fundamentally, the experience of our being grounded in God, rooted in him with absolute sureness and with a confidence that is always deepening because the depths of God can never by measured by humankind. This is the experience of prayer: the experience of falling into love, into the depths of love with complete trust, with a complete "letting go." To say that "God is the ground of our being" is not an abstract, metaphysical concept. It is the statement that our reality derives from his being the one Reality, our being from his being Being itself. To be open to this as the great fact of our life and existence we have to approach our prayer with confidence.

But confidence is something modern man is trained to distrust. The proper, respectable, scientific attitude is scepticism. Because scientific explanations of natural phenomena change so rapidly in the light of new knowledge it seems that any understanding we may have of ourselves or the human situation can only have limited and temporary validity. Consequently, our time has become an age of the half-hearted commitment, the other half holding on to scepticism, self-analysis, keeping one's options open. This would have something to recommend it if it led to happiness, to richness, or breadth of experience. But, as we all know, when we hold ourselves back on the brink of commitment we find ourselves increasingly enmeshed by a sense of isolation, of discontent, of anxious, vague desire. And we know that on those occasions we have had the courage to let go we have found ourselves unexpectedly, even miraculously borne up again. The act of faith, of generous self-commitment, is the context in which we know the power of transcendence. In committing ourselves we are lifted above ourselves, out of the prison of our self-consciousness and beyond our limitations. This is what St. Peter means by being "alive with the life of God" (1 Pet. 4:6) and what St. Paul means by attaining to "fullness of being, the fullness of God himself" (Eph. 3:19). In transcending ourselves, which we do with the power of the risen, transcendent Christ, we are led into oneness with our Source and Father.

The first step in this process of transcendence and union with God is made when we turn to prayer. This is a moment of truth. It is a moment when we are confronted with the fact of our own existence and are challenged to accept the gift of it with utter generosity and simplicity. It is a moment of silence and a moment of love. We have, in this moment of decision, to turn with a faith that allows us to turn aside from everything. This is the abandonment, the letting go of prayer. It is casting out into the depth of God as the ground of our being and allowing ourselves to fall back into our source. It can seem—because of the language we have to use to describe it—as a retrogressive movement. We call it a "going back," a "returning." And in a sense it is. It is the returning home of the prodigal son who understood that his reality was to be found at home and not in the restless pursuit of illusion abroad. The monastic Fathers used to describe it as a wandering in a land of "unlikeness" and a return to our real likeness as image of God. This aspect of prayer as a restoration, a returning or homecoming, is profoundly important to us. It emphasizes the humanity of the journey we are all called to make and it suggests some of the tenderest and most intimate reasons that God is known to us, and described by Jesus to us as "Father."

But the journey is also, and equally, a progression. We are not merely recovering a lost innocence. We are growing into innocence, becoming more like our Father who leads us into the universal maturity of Jesus, "shaped to the likeness of his Son, that he might be the eldest among a large family of brothers" (Rom. 8:29). It is when we glimpse this dynamic of prayer as progression through return that we find the only ultimate assurance there is, which is the assurance of Being-in-love with God. Because of this confidence in their own reality, men and women of faith are quite surefooted in their act of abandonment. Their security and confidence derive not from external forms or internal concepts but from the fact that our center of gravity is found not merely in our own ephemeral experience but in the experience of God himself. God's experience of himself, wholly undifferentiated, is the Spirit: the love of the Father for the Son and reciprocal love of the Son for the Father. The simple and indescribable wonder of the Christian life is that each of us and all of us together are called to enter this selfsame experience "in the Spirit."

We find the courage to be in entering the transcendent experience by which we are delivered from our limitations and are empowered with the liberty of God. Our first Pope, Peter, whom we encounter in the New Testament as such a lovable and fallible man, puts it in such daring and confident words that we have to be constantly reminded that they apply to each one of us: "His divine power has bestowed on us everything that makes for life and true religion, enabling us to know the One who called us by his own splendor and might. Through his might and splendor he has given us his promises, great beyond all price, and through them you may escape the corruption with which lust has infected the world, and come to share in the very being of God" (2 Pet. 1:3-4).

It is "sharing in the very being of God" that is the experience of our prayer. This is presented to us partly as a "promise," partly as an invitation, but also as a challenge. It is not enough for us to "take it or leave it," putting off the moment of response. Our capacity to respond—a capacity we have through the union of our spirit with the Spirit of Jesus—unfolds itself in our lives as a responsibility to attain to the full maturity of our humanity. Our society trains us to remain childish, dependent on external stimuli and amusement, spoon-fed on the prepackaged experiences we call entertainment that have as much spiritual nutrition as the convenience foods that, like television, symbolize our culture. In discovering the existence of such a responsibility in our lives we are tempted and trained to evade it, to retreat yet again into childish distraction and dissipation. The responsibility of making a mature response seems to us like a curtailment of our freedom.

This is why meditation is so important for us all. It prepares us for the real freedom that lives and rejoices at the heart of this mystery of love within us, the movement of divine energy that is also the stillness of our pilgrimage of faith. To pray in the infinite depths of our spirit, which is the depth of God, is to be utterly free. And our daily meditation, the deepening experience that flowers on the trellis of our discipline, teaches us the essential lesson of maturity: freedom does not consist in doing what we want but in being who we are. To be free is to have been liberated into being by a power of love greater than our own power of ego. It is to have encountered and responded to the Other in humility. The liberty is the liberty to be open to God as the ground of our being—the structure of all reality, inner and outer. It is to be redeemed by love from the slavery of self-consciousness and self-preoccupation.

Language, by itself, is very frustrating because it has so inbuilt a dimension of ambiguity. It is not an uncommon experience to talk to someone about this need to be less self-preoccupied and to find that the talking is only making him or her more so. We all have this fatal capacity for spiritual ambiguity, for self-deception. The heart has to pass through many mirages before we reach the threshold of love at its center.

What will lead us through the desert of self-deception and through all the evaporating illusions of double meaning? "Blessed are the poor in spirit for theirs is the Kingdom of Heaven. Blessed are the pure in heart for they shall see God." The joy of the Kingdom accepts no compromises. It is all-compassionate and all-forgiving but it demands not less than everything. In meditating with all the faith, simplicity, and childlike generosity we are capable of, we begin to give everything. The more we do give the more is demanded from us. This reveals itself not as a tyranny but as a wonderful grace, deepening us and liberating the spiral of being that the ego has kept repressed. The more we give the more is asked because the more we give the more we have, and "to him who has more will be given." Nothing can show us better the dynamism of love at the heart of life than this paradox of giving and receiving, having and renouncing, possession and dispossession. It is the dynamic of the "very being of God."

The way into this dynamism is the way of simplicity and poverty. It is learning to say our word, our mantra. Learning to say it is learning to turn aside from that very self-consciousness and self-preoccupation that complicates us and loads us down with the riches that prevent us from becoming conscious of the Spirit within us, alive and active in our inmost centers. The "riches" that the Gospel tells us make it so difficult to enter the Kingdom are the limited, incomplete truths that result from our self-analysis. We have to understand with simple clarity that self-analysis is not self-knowledge nor is it even the way to self-knowledge. The little half-truths our self-analysis reveal are merely refractions of the great, single, simple, and central truth. To know ourselves we have to turn wholly away from all self-preoccupation and even from those ways in which we are self-conscious. This is the great poverty of Christ centered in the Father who sent him and spoke through him (John 8:28). It is the great poverty, the great richness and generosity of the mantra. No one should ever say this is easy. Nor should anyone say it is impossible for anyone. It demands only faith. To know ourselves means to discover our selves in another. Our ultimate self-knowledge, which is the Spirit of Christ united to our spirit, means discovering ourselves in God. But to turn from self involves courage because it can seem as if we are turning away from all we have and know toward nothing, only to find that we have lost ourself and gained nothing. "No man can be a follower of mine unless he leave self behind and follow me." Every act of faith is a step into the infinite expanse of God.

Faced with this challenge to Be, people can react by making an image of God from their own self-conscious preoccupations and addressing themselves to this image, talking to it, "listening" to it. People are even advised to talk over their problems with God. Hearing this sort of advice I can only recall the words of Jesus:

> In your prayers do not go babbling on like the heathen who imagine the more they say the more likely they are to be heard. Do not imitate them. Your Father knows what your needs are before you ask him. This is how you should pray. . .
> (Matt. 6:7-9)

Jesus then gave his followers the seven, short rhythmical phrases for their prayer that we know as the Lord's Prayer. Jesus's teaching on prayer emphasizes for us time and again that prayer is always a growth in selflessness, in simplicity, in unity of consciousness with the Spirit.

There is another way we can react to (or rather, evade) this challenge to Be. We can accept that we have to renounce multiplicity of thought and imagination but then just set off wandering in the labyrinthine ways of our psyches, savoring our own experiences, setting our own courses, acting as our own guides. This is to be more turned upon ourselves than ever, more than ever turned away from the inner guide that is the Spirit whom we find by turning from self-centeredness and from the outer guide that is our Christian tradition.

The pilgrimage of prayer is followed between these two dead ends of illusion: "talking your problems over" is always likely to lead you deeper into ego fixation, and drifting in an undisciplined self-observation is likely to isolate you more effectively from God, from others, from yourself. This is why the simplicity and the poverty of the mantra is so vital to the pilgrimage of meditation. In saying it with fidelity we are doing all we are called to do, which is to turn from self. The rest we leave to the free gift of God, without desire or expectation. We begin in faith. We continue in faith. In faith we arrive. Our opportunity and our responsibility is to be self-emptying disciples of our Master. A disciple is not greater than his master. It is enough that we should become like him. Our way to imitate his wholehearted *kenosis*, his self-emptying, is the way of prayer. It is a real journey we are on, with real demands and a real realization. And so we must really be faithful to our word: not just thinking of saying it but saying it with simplicity and love.

The reality of God is like a sea. Isolated from reality, we are like people standing on the shore. Some sit, like King Canute, ordering the tide to turn back. Others gaze romantically at its beauty and vastness from a safe distance. But we are all called to be baptized, to be plunged into it and to allow its all-powerful tide to direct our lives. To do this we have to leave our familiar dry shore and travel to the further shore of our origin. The poverty and joy of our word leads us into the sea and, once there, it keeps us simply in the current of the Spirit that leads us to a place unknown to us where we know ourselves in Him, in His eternal now.

Our call is so deep and so wonderful. No fear or self-preoccupation should hinder our response. I send you our support and encouragement on the journey we share and urge you to ever more self-emptying discipleship of our Lord. May we grow into his full maturity and in his selflessness and love and so enter more fully into the power of love between him and our Father, which is the Spirit we share.

With much love,

John Main, OSB

Letter Eight (AUGUST 1979)

In the weeks between our June and August newsletters we heard that the two properties on the island of Montreal that we had been considering for our move and expansion were to be taken over by the city authorities. So we were back at the beginning of our search and with more reason every day for expansion. What we were looking for was not, of course, easily found: a property with some agricultural potential, a large central house, and two or three smaller cottages or barns. We would have to extend our search further west and off the island. But we still meant to be within easy reach of the city to which our monastic life and prayer could continue to be of service and relevance. Our plan, too, was to keep on the Vendôme center for the weekly groups and as a place of continuous prayer in the heart of the city. Until the day that it might become a monastic house of studies as well, it could be run by a resident lay community as an extension or sphere of the monastery.

Our plans, of course, would have to depend on the situation as it developed in practice. And for the time being the situation took me to give the community retreat at St. Peter's Abbey in Saskatchewan. In July I spent a few days at Antigonish, Nova Scotia, at a conference of sisters from the Congregation de Notre Dame gathered by the theme of "prayer in a life of service" from across Canada and the United States. The Mother house of the C.N.D. in Montreal had shown us great kindness from our earliest days in giving us furniture and equipment for our house and they were continuing to support us now that we planned our next stage of growth.

Among our visitors during this period was Dom Jean Leclercq, the Benedictine scholar of Clairvaux in Luxembourg, who came to see us with the committee of the Canadian Union of Contemplative Religious. We discussed together the theme of the conference they were planning to hold in 1980 — the forms of contemplative life relevant to our times and the role of the liturgy in the monastic life. Dom Leclercq's worldwide experience of contemporary monasticism confirmed our own insights gained in Montreal and London. The religious life would survive vitally only where there was a shifting of the monk's center of consciousness from external work and worship to a more deeply interior source, where the axis of his life would be the journey into the mystery of God—his inner journey of prayer. It was not easy to find the right form of expression for this conviction. To many religious it would perhaps sound extremist and an undervaluation of monastic service to the world in education or in the missionary field. It was refreshing and encouraging to talk to Dom Leclercq and his companions and to find out that we shared a practical and balanced conviction that, far from restricting its development, the restoration of the contemplative priority to monasticism would set it free, as it had perhaps never been free before, to serve the world in the world's deepest contemporary need.

We enjoyed a second and longer visit from Bishop Henry Hill, who spent a two-week retreat with us, working, praying, and sharing his wide experience of different Christian communions.

In August Brother Laurence traveled south to visit the Monastery of Christ in the Desert in New Mexico, a small community like ours associated with Mount Saviour. On his way back home he visited the charismatic Benedictine Abbey at Pecos and brought back to us a vivid account of the range of Benedictine life that these two communities witnessed to within a hundred miles of each other.

A further dimension of the generosity of the influence of the Rule of Benedict was opened up when, at the end of August, we met with Bede Griffiths at the end of his U.S. lecture tour. During the few days we spent at Mount Saviour with him and Brother Amaldas of his community, he spoke of the courageous and troubled founding of his Benedictine ashram in southern India by Father Monchanin and Dom Henri le Saux (Abhishiktananda). Of particular interest to us were the discussions we shared on the state of Western monasticism and Father Bede's own belief that the contemplative life in the West would be revived through networks of small ashramic-type monasteries located in the main population centers as a living witness to the journey from self to God.

August 24, 1979

My Dearest Friends,

Greetings in the Lord.

Our life since we last wrote to you has been a rich and a full one. We have looked forward to telling you something of it in this letter and to share with you some of the insights we have gained through those we have met away or who have visited us here. As you know, we try to make these letters more than just lists of news items and so we give a kind of representative selection of the events in our life. We also try to make them something less than homilies and so the reflections we share with you we try to keep in the context of our daily life.

The ordinariness of life—not its dullness—is the necessary context in which our deeper experience can be assimilated and so lead the whole persons we are to fullness of being. Thus it is that if you and we alike become wiser in time it is through experience and practice rather than through mere abstraction and theory. There is no wisdom that is not the "wisdom of humility"—none that is not the result of loving more deeply and allowing ourselves to be loved more vulnerably.

In July I spent some days at a conference of C.N.D. sisters and we spoke of the need to clarify our vision of prayer as the basis of every apostolic work. To all of us it seemed important to go beyond the conventional division of the Christian life into "active" and "contemplative." The Christian is not developing a narrow specialization in order to become an "expert" in prayer in the fullness and balance of the humanity of Christ, the Man who is fully alive to God in all things. Of course, each one finds this wholeness in a unique blend of silence and speech, stillness and action. Indeed, our lifetime is, in essence, the progressive discovery and realization of this blend—becoming the person we are called to be.

We find our true selves, our unique participation in the Body, only through finding our own inner balance and harmony. If we lose touch with the creative poise of the *via media* in the Christian life, then we inevitably distort our humanity and all we do suffers distortion. The gospel does not instruct us to choose exclusively either to work with the poor or to undertake the contemplative journey. It tells of getting lost in the breadth of possibility this open command lays before us—its challenge. Confusion results from evasion. We find the balance as a gift by facing and generously responding to the present moment. We do not create the balance out of our own resources. All is given and we simply have to learn to be openhearted in responding to the gift.

Of course to talk of this and to do it is not the same thing. At

Antigonish it was a great joy to be able to do both. The group of us who discussed these issues and felt the great challenge facing the religious life today were also able to turn aside from the talking and the generalizing and to become silent as we meditated together each day. The exchanges we had in discussion were enriching but the silence was pure gold.

One weekend we were happily surprised to hear from Dom Jean Leclercq. At a meeting he had recently attended they had discussed the great challenges facing the religious life at the present time. The central challenge they saw was finding the way to present the perennial call to transcendence of self to so self-conscious a generation as our own.

It is so obvious that we cannot rest content with forms and formulas but we must be on the pilgrimage to find ways of speaking to contemporary men and women at the profoundest levels. One thing clear to us all was that we will have to reassess the place of liturgical prayer in our lives. And it was felt very deeply that if the contemplative life is to survive—and more than survive, to flourish so that it can be at the service of the Church—then it has to recover the absolute contemplative experience that lies, as it were, latent in our orders and congregations, planted there so often by the founders and foundresses and so often covered up or lost in the wake of expansion.

Recovering the contemplative roots of our great orders is, however, much more than a question of academic research or experimentation with different methods or techniques. It demands both the willingness to be taught by one's own tradition, to be a disciple of a living tradition, and to persevere in the ordinariness of the commitment such discipleship entails. We are all too capable of many "first fervors of conversion," as St. Benedict calls it in the prologue to his Rule; and we can too easily make a spiritual supermarket out of the tradition, keeping ourselves supplied with novelties and special offers. Talking to Dom Leclercq and learning from his wide experience of the Church and its monastic life around the world, it became clear how immediate is this challenge to be truly serious—a challenge the Vatican Council and the teaching Church put clearly before her religious communities. We can be blinded to the immediacy of the situation by the impressive institutional structures that still remain around us. But structures without a living Spirit issuing from committed and open hearts too easily become preoccupied with self-survival rather than with transcendence of self. We must learn from our experience in prayer that our call is to follow Christ in death to self and in resurrection to new, unlimited life in him, with him, and through him.

In July we also had the great personal delight of a visit from Bishop Henry Hill, the Anglican Bishop of Ontario. We talked together daily of the other great challenge facing the Church in the West, that of her own unity as a concerted witness to the one Lord that the different Christian communions serve. The many theological and ecumenical conferences have brought us a long way toward this essential unity, but they can only serve a limited need. What, by their nature, they cannot do is lead us beyond the multiplicity of concepts into the simplicity of God and the unity of his transcendent love found in and through Jesus.

Again, it seemed to us as we spoke that the challenge facing the larger community is the same facing each of us. Indeed, we belong to a community because we are each a microcosm of it. And our challenge as we return daily to meditate is to lay down everything we are, our very selves, before the infinite mystery of God. The ideas and experience that bring us to this moment of prayer ("the sacrifice of mind and heart") are renounced together with all psychological self-reflection and theological speculation. The great achievements in ecumenical theological understanding over the past twenty years are only fulfilled by leading us beyond the fascination of differences to the celebration of likenesses, from the conference room to the prayer room, from words to the Word spoken to all people in silence. As with the renewal of the religious life in the Church, the challenge of Christian unity is already upon us, demanding that we recognize and respond to the moments of grace that are opportunities for real prayer in real communion. During Bishop Hill's stay it was a joy and a privilege for us to recognize such a moment.

Our last piece of news takes up the theme of the other meetings of the summer. On August 20 we went to Mount Saviour to meet with Dom Bede Griffiths, who was to spend a few days of quiet there after his lecture tour of American monasteries. I had last met Father Bede when he was a monk of Prinknash Abbey in England, but for the past twenty-five years he has been in India working toward the growth of a truly Indian-Christian monastic life. In discussion with the Community at Mount Saviour, he spoke to us of the essential unity of the monastic order in all its manifestations around the world—a unity deriving from the monk's essential task and calling, his search for God.

It seemed evident to us that the life of a religious community truly centered in Christ has to be a life centered on meditation. To the vast majority of Indians, he told us, the Church in India is seen as a wonderful worker in the social field, but it has not been to the Church that they go to be led into the life of the spirit. The thousands of young Westerners who travel to the East go seeking a living experience of the mystery of God they could not find in the Church in the West. Some, no doubt, do find genuine guides and teachers of prayer with whom they can, if they are serious themselves, learn to meditate. But many others do not have such fortune and are left confused and even more alienated than before. It is clear that these young people do not reject God. Why have they then rejected the Christian religious structure of the West?

Perhaps the reason is that we in the West have become too religious rather than truly spiritual. What so many today are seeking is a humble yet authoritative witness to the absolute. Our call as monks is always a call to the experience of God in Christ. This experience has to be personal if it is to be real. Our contemporaries in the West will only come to our monasteries when they are convinced that this is the primary reason for our existence—that we do truly seek God as our very first responsibility.

Our essential ideal is union—within ourselves, with others, with God. One side of us seeks to preserve our alienation, but our "Godlikeness" is stronger than this egoism and leaves us restless until we achieve communion. Religion has the essential function of continually reminding us that we will achieve our ideal only by first entering our own mystery, traveling to the ground of our being where we find ourselves simply as we are.

From that point of personal integration radiates the power of union with others and with God—the power that is simply the power of love, of God who is Love. In the depth of our being we are relentlessly summoned to realize our union with the Spirit of God in whom we have our being.

It is a mysterious sign of our age that this intuition is accepted without question by so many of the thousands who seek the way outside conventional religion. They have leaped back in a moment to a basic spiritual truth that centuries of organized religion have obscured for so many. It must, then, be as absurd to them as it was to St. Paul to find Christians "morbidly keen on mere verbal questions and quibbles" (1 Tim. 5:6) that lead us to lose grip of the Truth. Religion without spiritual experience becomes atrophied and futile, as St. James realized (James 1:26). But to place meditation at the center of our religious life is not to deny the value of religion. As St. Paul knew also, it affirms it: of course religion does yield high dividends, he tells us—but only to the individuals whose resources are within them (1 Tim. 6:6).

What our encounter with India and the East is teaching us is something we should never have forgotten—that the essential Christian experience is beyond the capacity of any cultural or intellectual form to express. This is the "glorious liberty of the children of God": no restriction. It became so clear to us talking with Father Bede that this experience has to be restored to the heart of the Church if she is to face creatively the challenges before her: the challenge of the renewal of her contemplative religious life, the challenge of finding unity in the Spirit with all Christian communions, the challenge of embracing the non-Christian religions with the universal love of Christ present in the hearts of all people and which she has a special duty to release and identify. To meet these challenges each one of us must be personally rooted in the experience of God that Jesus personally knows and shares with us all through his Spirit.

We do not earn this experience or create it from our own resources; it is for us to prepare for the grace of its giving. Our fidelity to meditation is our preparation, our patient and ever deepening openness to the mystery that fills and contains us. We have to be still. We have to be silent. We have to stand reverently in the cave of our hearts, the palace of God's kingdom within us.

To meditate is just to "stand still in the center." The very word "meditation" is made up from the Latin words *stare in medio*, to abide in the center. But it seems inadequate to say this is just "centering ourselves" or even "finding our center." We do this too, but not if it is our conscious aim—that would be too self-conscious, too desiring. We find our center only by placing ourselves in the silence of God beyond any image of center or circumference. What we think of as "our" center is too often an illusion of the self-reflecting ego, somewhere we like to take up our stand and observe God at work in us. But this can never be the way.

Our fear of union, of the loss of self and finding of self in the otherness of God, is so unfounded. Yet it often dispels the Spirit in individuals, in communities, and in Churches who fear to lose either their personality, their distinctiveness, or their exclusiveness. But the wonder of union is precisely that it does *not* obliterate, but is creative. Not that it absorbs, but that it recreates. To be involved is to evolve. Teilhard de Chardin puts it beautifully and simply when he says, "Union differentiates." In union the rich variety of the human mystery is apprehended as a reflection of the unbounded creativity of God.

The challenges that face us point to the mystery of union we are summoned to enter. But we find our way into this mystery of union with others and with God only when we reach in ourselves that place where Jesus experiences his oneness with the Father. That place from which he prayed, "I in them and thou in me, that they may become perfectly one."

Our communities of prayer, large and small, and each of us on our unique pilgrimage of faith participate in the building up of the unified Body. Whether we can know or understand it at all, we are all invited to enter into the communion within God himself. This communion we enter through the Spirit who breathes freely in the open spaces of our hearts.

We keep you in our heart.

With much love,

John Main, OSB

Letter Nine (OCTOBER 1979)

For some time I had been having some pain and when I was examined, it was discovered that surgery was necessary. It happened at the worst possible time as Brother Laurence was shortly to make his solemn monastic profession at Mount Saviour. My sudden departure for the hospital placed many extra responsibilities on his shoulders, not the least of which was the continued leadership of the community and the meditation groups.

He had been ordained to Minor Orders as the first step toward his ordination to the priesthood in early September. Bishop Crowley had come to us at Vendôme for Compline and meditation and bestowed the orders at a ceremony at which several of our friends participated. It also fell to Brother Laurence to greet our former Abbot from Ealing who flew over from England to attend his profession and to meet our new brethren at Mount Saviour. Bishop Crowley also participated in the ceremony and led a group of our friends from Montreal down to Elmira, New York.

In addition, Brother Laurence brought out the next newsletter, using some material from a talk I had given to the Anglican Bishops of Eastern Canada in Quebec City in September. He gave news of our guests, who had been many and various old friends from the seminary in Toronto, a missionary doctor on leave from Uganda, an English monk studying monastic liturgy in North America, and a Philippino Sister preparing to return home. At the end of August I had given a retreat at the Cloister in Maryknoll and spoken on meditation to the Knights of Malta at St. Benoit du Lac, the large Benedictine Abbey about a hundred miles from Montreal.

October 9, 1979

Dear Friends,

Peace and love in the Lord.

Father John was about to prepare this newsletter when we learned of a serious medical problem he has which requires surgery.

The substance of this letter will be taken from notes Father John prepared for a talk he gave to a group of Anglican Bishops and their advisors in Quebec City in September and from notes for his proposed talks to the Lakeshore School.

When he was in Quebec City, Father John spoke of the vision of the Church that has begun to emerge from the contemplative experience of our time. It is difficult, he said, to generalize about the state of the Church today, covering as it does such a spectrum of belief and devotion. But what the rich variety of the Christian communions do reveal today more clearly than in the past is that the mystery of the Church is the mystery of personhood. Out of every area of Christian thought and activity today there comes the same insistence that abstract or legalistic answers to the riddles of our lives are inadequate. Rulebook regulations applied wihtout human compassion for the uniqueness of each individual are as futile as the neat intellectual formulas that have no integral power to change the way we live. But, he went on, the risk we run in giving due supremacy to the personal criterion of truth is that it can lead us into mere subjectivism or self-indulgence without the discipline, the teaching, of the tradition. One of the most damaging divisions in our fractured society is the split made between personal experience and tradition. What the Church is empowered to proclaim out of the vitality and freshness of her knowledge of the Person of Christ—which is her corporate contemplative experience as the Body of Christ—is that in the moment of pure love experience and tradition are one.

The mystery of God is available to humankind in the mystery of the Person of Jesus. It is a living mystery, overflowing the normal limits of our thought and feeling just as it transcends any human organization that tries to contain or control it. It is a mystery greater than each of us and greater than all of us, yet one to which we are closer than we are to ourselves because it contains us. The immanence and transcendence of the mystery, like the realities of tradition and experience, are seen as one in the moment of contemplative vision when, loving so generously that we rise above ourselves, we see no longer with our own eyes but enter into the vision of God.

We can know all this conceptually inasmuch as we can put it into words. But how satisfied are we at the end of all our word making? Don't we feel only more deeply impelled to enter into a direct, undifferentiated experience—*the* experience itself? It is this response that leads to full personhood—both realizing and accepting generously that although the mystery lies beyond our power to understand it does not lie beyond our experience. Indeed, we are each of us summoned by the very fact of our creation to experience it. What this demands simply is the courage of love. What it means simply is being fully human, fully alive.

Simone Weil has said that goodness can only be known in the act of goodness, never in anticipation or in retrospect. What she was saying rather abstractly is what every human being (and in particular every child) knows from his or her own experience. The difference is between thinking of someone and being with them; between looking forward to an experience and being inside the experience; between image and object, illusion and reality. What is so astounding is that once we have left the relative simplicity of childhood behind us we so easily forget this and become idea-centered rather than experience-centered. The difficulty facing all teachers in the Church is to convince people that this is not esoteric knowledge but plain simplicity. A group of children who come to our monastery in Montreal to meditate each week could really communicate this so much better by their silence and fidelity to the adult groups than all of us put together.

What I am suggesting is this: our society has become personalistic after a long history of dominant legalism and intellectualism. But at the same time it has lost a vital contact with its tradition and so it is pursuing an experience-centered course, not bad in itself as I have said, but presently lacking the stability and centrality the tradition can give it. What the Church must proclaim is that this tradition is the central human experience of the Mystery writ large. To be in contact with the tradition is not to forego the validity of our own experience but to have the grace of the opportunity to make our experience complete—by making it other-centered, purifying it of all egoism, all self-preoccupation. The tradition—and this is the community of the faithful as the Person of Christ—is the universal hinge upon which we swing away from ourselves to God. At no time in history has the richness of this tradition been more universally available to us. Why, then, do we remain so trapped in the prison of our ego and why does our experience, deep as it is, fail to reach its full potential in the vision of God—no longer "seeing God" but being robed in the power of God's vision?

We all know of people who have had visions. I do not at all doubt their sincerity. But my own conviction, in the teaching of the tradition, is that the greatest enemy of *oratio pura*—simple prayer as our participation in Christ's experience of God—is our imagination. I have tried to find ways of putting this more palatably to people who are shocked or offended by what seems to them an insult to their humanity. But I do believe, and believe it is the belief of the tradition (experience and tradition being one again) that the more we "think" about God, picture him, or stir up our imagination for autonomous visions of him, the less we can experience him. This is not to denigrate theology, philosophy, or art. But these three fruits of our minds and hearts have value for ultimate meaning only so far as they clarify, encourage, or purify our journey to the frontiers of the limited human consciousness. On this frontier we are met by a guide, who is unlimited consciousness, the Person of Jesus Christ. We reach this frontier only if we travel light, if we have left all behind us and if we embrace the one who meets us with absolute trust. At that moment we know from our own experience that he is the Way, the Truth, and the Life.

The deep spiritual search of our contemporaries is for this personal experience that authenticates them in relation to the

Absolute. In St. Paul's words, they are seeking "justification." The danger we face in this search is that it has lost its stabilizing contact with the common tradition and therefore so often leads straight back to self-obsession and self-indulgence by way of the easy options of religious nostalgia or legalism. The Church must provide the centrality of insight and teaching that will prevent this for we can ill afford further delays in an effective proclamation of the Kingdom. And what she must proclaim, from the rich depth and variety of her tradition, is that this search for the authentic experience of God is her foremost concern and is, indeed, the only valid reason for her existence.

It is not enough for us to talk about the mystery of God in Jesus. We have to talk from *within* the heart of the mystery where we are led by the Spirit. Any talking secondhand will fail to communicate the life-giving word and instead merely provide definitions and dogma. But if we have allowed ourselves to be led into the secret of Christ-within-us, we will speak with power—for it will not be us speaking but the Spirit speaking through us. This is experience, not theory—personal knowledge, not ideology.

Of course, we all know that the last ten or fifteen years have shown that the search for experience out of context only leads back deeper into the labyrinth of egoism. The desire to possess one's experience, to hoard or cultivate it, that has characterized part of our modern culture so strongly—and is a perennial part of human nature—is ultimately self-defeating. We can only be joyful if, in Blake's phrase, we "kiss the joy as it flies." If we bind it to ourselves we kill it.

The context for all authentic personal experience that leads to the redemptive moment of transcendence is our own tradition. And this is why St. Paul says we are authenticated, "justified," by faith. We have come to think of faith merely in terms of knowledge—we say someone has a "good grasp of faith," meaning he or she is well read in scripture or theology. And, in a way, faith is knowledge. But not our knowledge. It is the knowledge Jesus enjoys of his Father. It is the communion of love that is God's knowledge of himself, so personal that it is the Holy Spirit. We are redeemed from the limitations of our narrow selves into the glorious liberty of those born of God by our personal contact with this self-knowledge of God. It is not a contact we can have from the outside, touching God as an object, but only from within God himself. This is possible for man because Jesus is the innerness of God, his self-revelation. To know him is to know the Father. To be open to him is to expand far beyond the frontiers of our self-regarding consciousness into communion with his consciousness, unlimited and fully human.

This is the knowledge beyond knowing that St. Paul urged the early Christians to accept. It is the secret of faith and the living power of the tradition that has been passed on in the loving community of the faithful from the first century to our own. It is a knowledge that is forever present, always unchanging, and ever expanding because it is within the infinite mystery of the God who Is. To possess this knowledge is to allow oneself to be possessed by the infinite love of God and to find oneself again, transformed into servants of that love. We love one another because "we possess the mind of Christ."

I hope this serves, as Father John's other letters have, to encourage all of us to deepen our poverty and fidelity on the pilgrimage we follow together, in obedience to the Lord's will for each of us.

Please keep Father John in your hearts.

We send our love,

Laurence Freeman, OSB

Letter Ten (DECEMBER 1979)

B y the time of the next newsletter, my convalescence was proceeding smoothly, so much so that my doctor described me as a "textbook recovery." By mid-December I was able to relieve Brother Laurence of some of the responsibilities he had been carrying since I had gone into hospital.

On Sunday, December 9, Brother Laurence was ordained to the diaconate by Bishop Crowley. The ceremony took place at the Atwater chapel and about two hundred of our friends and many from the groups took part in the liturgy to make it a deeply prayerful and fraternal moment in the history of our community. The Bishop spoke of the mystery of the Church that becomes visible in the calling forth of one of its members for special service to the community of the faithful. Many of those present knew personally how appropriate it was at this time that Brother Laurence, who had given so much of himself to the community and the groups, should have his generous service sacramentalized in the diaconate.

Our guests had continued to enrich our life both by the perspective they opened up on our work and the sharing of their own insights or traditions. A Unitarian minister and chaplain at Cornell University visited us and discussed the familiar problems of communicating our own tradition of meditation to contemporaries so alienated from the discipline of any tradition. We also welcomed Father Placid from Mount Saviour, who had been cofounder of the monastery with Damasus Winzen, and, like ourselves, originally a monk of the English congregation.

The priests' group had continued to meet faithfully with a core of six to seven members every week for the past year and a half. In early December they spent a day with us in prayer and discussion, turning to the question that had been concerning it for some time of how to communicate its experience and conviction about meditation to its fellow-priests. We agreed the only effective communication could be made if they were to spend two or three days together, not just talking of prayer, but together entering the silence of prayer. It was thus decided to arrange a retreat of this kind in the Spring.

Another new venture was the formation of a Benedictine Oblate group, which the newsletter described and took as its theme. The relationship of an Oblate to a monastery offered a traditional way of developing our own monastic witness to the world—a witness to a pilgrimage all men and women follow together, whatever their condition in life. The ceremony of receiving Oblate novices for a year before their oblation underlined the spiritual participation in the monastic journey, and the presentation of a copy of the Rule and the Medal of St. Benedict symbolized their entrance into the Benedictine tradition. Rooted in this by their twice-daily meditation, they would come to share in their own experience of St. Benedict's vision of the harmony of prayer and work. Our first Oblate was Rosie Lovat, received on the last day of her month's stay with us, and it seemed right to all of us that she should be the first Oblate as she has given so much of herself and so generously to the community from the beginning. Two days later Bishop Hill became our first ecumenical Oblate, followed soon by Louis Chavez, a young married man working in the civil service in Toronto.

My illness had given me more time for reflection and soon, too, for writing. At my doctor's advice I was leaving Montreal for the sun in January and would be staying in a monastery in Nassau to complete my recovery. While there, I would be able to write in person to all those who had sent me good wishes as well as bring some thoughts together on the way our community would grow in the decade we were about to enter.

December 18, 1979

My Dearest Friends,

How good it is to be able to write to you again. After a serious operation, when we sail close to the perimeters of life and death, we have a finer perception of life as a sheer gift. We feel more deeply and clearly the presence of the beauty and goodness that give depth of meaning to our life. I am so full of thanks that I am able to write once more and so full of gratitude to all of you who have kept me in your hearts during these days of my recovery.

I am pleased to tell you that as a result of the wonderful care I have received from all the community, I have made an excellent recovery and now feel stronger and better than I have for months past. This is especially good as we are moving into a period of much development in our foundation, as we seek to expand and make firm the growth of the community.

Dom Laurence made his Solemn Profession at Mount Saviour Monastery in New York State on October 18. Prior Martin Boler received his vows and presided at the Mass of his Profession. Bishop Crowley of Montreal concelebrated at the Mass along with our former abbot, who came from Ealing to be present at this first Solemn Profession for our community. Several members of the community and friends from Montreal also travelled to Mount Saviour to share in the occasion.

In December I participated for a morning in a conference of the Heads of Anglican Theological Colleges from across Canada. It was a challenging experience to try to share with this influential group my convictions about formation in prayer. What I tried to say to the group was that I considered the leading of theological students into the simple experience of pure prayer as the essential foundation of their professional formation. What I tried to stress was that this is the essential discipline of Christian discipleship, the essential learning process of becoming Christlike. This demands of us a reevaluation of what we mean by discipleship and a reaffirmation of our understanding of discipline: it is both the discipline of the tradition that we must study and understand and be rooted in as genuine witnesses to its truth; and also the discipline of daily renewal, the daily pilgrimage, that the real practice of the tradition involves. My own very strong conviction is that it is not enough for us to study the Christian faith or just to accept it. We must also come to experience the Christian truth ourselves, in ourselves. This is the foundational "knowledge" of the Christian way that St. Paul speaks about in his letter to the Ephesians.

*   *   *

These have been days of new planning and development and one thing I would like to tell you about is our establishment of a group of Oblates around the monastery. An Oblate is a person who shares the ideals of the community and seeks to follow these ideals in the circumstances of his or her own life. We hope to establish groups of Oblates in any place where there are sufficient interested people. The Oblate seeks to live by the spirit of the Rule of St. Benedict—a spirit characterized by its priority of love, generosity, liberty, and discretion and that seeks to realize and communicate the kingdom of peace. The Oblate joins the community in this spirit each day by saying the Morning Prayer and evening Vespers of our Office and, after each of these, spends a half an hour in meditation.

* * *

Taking the step to become an Oblate of St. Benedict is a movement toward the new life, which is the good news of the Gospel. In this Christmastide letter, in a time when we are all thinking of the new life of Christ and our own rebirth in grace as the result of his birth in the flesh, I thought it would be appropriate to put down before you some thoughts on the Spirit of St. Benedict, a spirit that flows so directly from a knowledge of the Incarnate Word born in us through the love of God.

For Benedict, the first quality we all require if we would respond to Christ and be open to his life in our hearts is the capacity to listen. The first word of the Rule is "Listen!" And as you all know, this capacity is one of the great fruits of meditation, which teaches us that the condition of true listening is silence. We can only listen to the word spoken to us by another if we ourselves are silent of all words. The wonder of Benedict's spirit as it speaks to us in the Rule is that his understanding of the prayerful heart is so naturally and humanly integrated into this whole vision of life. He does not see silence in the monastery, for example, just as a regulation to obeyed but wisely knows that there are times when charity will demand words. Instead, he sees silence as the fundamental condition of our heart, attentiveness to a reality larger than the limits of our immediate activities or concerns, a heart wrapped in silence and wholly attentive to the word of the Master. We are not attentive to this merely at set times: our attentiveness *is* the way we live, our silence is the state of being in which we respond to the gift of life. It is one of the great creative paradoxes of the Spirit that it is only in this attentive listening, this silent openness, that we can at all respond to the mystery of our experience with the appropriate response. Our busyness, our noisiness, our attempts to provide for all contingencies are all the ways we try to reduce the mystery of life to the status of a solvable problem—and in these ways we so often miss the creative moment, fail to see the gift as it opens before us. We lack the readiness on which the necessary spontaneity of spirit depends. We become dreamers of possibilities rather than tasters of real life.

Everyone is seeking a way. The problem is we so often demand to accept the way only on our own terms. We see ourselves as choosing God. We invite ourselves to the Master's banquet. And in doing so we are making an essentially immature response to the gift of our own being, a childish assessment of the infinite potential of the Life that has called us into being to share its own plenitude of joy. This is where our tradition is of such importance, why we have to know ourselves formed by and rooted in this progressive experience, why it has to be personally known and retransmitted with the genuineness of new discovery for every generation. The way of our tradition is a heart opened to the infinite mystery of God by awakening to itself. We awake in silence.

So often in the past I have urged you to be faithful to the recitation of your "one little word" in the time of your meditation, as the means of leaving behind all the noisiness of your own words and thoughts. At this time of Christmas—the time of the Incarnate Word—let me urge you to utter *faithfulness* during your morning and evening meditation: the word and only the word.

Part of the problem of our contemporaries in responding to such a simple teaching of the tradition is that we lack a confident vocabulary in which to describe our experience. We hesitate to be simple because we confuse simplicity with naivety, to be vulnerable because the catchword is "strength" or "self-sufficiency" and we think that vulnerability is weakness. Our religious vocabulary, which should at least help us to enter the realm of the silent and the inexpressible, has so often been made redundant. No word in this vocabulary is so much misunderstood by our contemporaries as "obedience." Generations of pious people have been brought up to believe it means merely "doing what you are told to do." Yet the Rule of St. Benedict links obedience to silence, to the mature condition of listening, in its opening words. It describes obedience as the glorious armor of the true child of God—or, in other words, as the way of standing steady in the knowledge of our true relationship to God, in the experience of receiving the gift of our own lives.

Obedience is nothing else than the capacity to listen to the other. In awaking to otherness we hear the word within which we ourselves come to be. We know the mystery that is our life as one that is simultaneously the mystery of sameness and of uniqueness. But we stray from God when we lose this attentiveness and no amount of talking or thinking about God can truly substitute to this openness to him. We stray by drowning out his Word with our own egotistical noisiness, the complex mirrorings of our imaginations. We stifle his life by our own self-fixation and by all manner of selfishness. The wise teaching of the Rule is that we are invited to return to him by obediential attentiveness. We are to be listeners. The Latin root of "obedience" is *ob-audire*, to hear, to listen. And the follower of Benedict is one who follows this teaching, committing himself or herself to the attitude and practice of listening, of attentiveness.

As you all know from your own experiences in prayer, our attentiveness is itself a journey—a journey into a wonderful and undreamed of realm of silence where for the first time we taste fullness of being. And you know that we learn attentiveness only with faithfulness of our daily practice. The early monks often saw this faithful regularity of the return to prayer as the means of bringing out the spark of God from stony hearts. St. Benedict, inheriting their teaching and retransmitting it, calls on his monks in the beginning of the Rule to "open their eyes to the Divine light"—and this is not as a casual option but as their first responsibility. It is the responsibility that falls on each of us if we are to respond to our existence and become the person we are called to be. Through Jesus we know that this responsibility is no burden but a gift and calling that should fill us with joy.

Our regularity and faithfulness to meditation brings the whole of this mystery closer and closer to us. At first we hear of it as something remote, alien, or for others. Then we see it as relevant to ourselves personally but like a distant mountain peak, beautiful but unattainable. Our journey is one that takes us away from this mistake of objectifying the mystery, of seeing it at all as something outside ourselves—although it may be easier to see it as remote and unreachable. Our faithfulness brings image and object ever closer together, into their true, undifferentiated union. Our journey brings us closer to our selves. The light to which St. Benedict urges us to open our eyes is in our hearts and the light *is* Christ. The wonder of our pilgrimage of prayer is that this discovery is itself the way we travel and our journey is into an ever richer realization of the mystery that can never be fathomed and can never be forgotten, for it is the mystery of the God who IS. The wonder, too, is that if only we will undertake the journey seriously, then once we find this light in our own hearts we have found it in the hearts of all. This is why St. Benedict makes this journey the indispensable foundation of his communities. One of the great mysteries of the experience of prayer is that is the only true foundation of a vital Christian community built up by people who, in awakening to this light in their heart, have awakened to themselves and to others.

Our journey into deeper attentiveness, the silence of our meditation, also brings us closer to the personal mystery of the *Church*. This is another religious word that has somehow lost its power to mediate any depth of meaning to our contemporaries. A word full of wonder, it has become bankrupt and only a more vital return to the experience it signifies will restore its meaning.

It means the community of the faithful. But only those who have the experience of being faithful can discover their communion and mediate this meaning. No community just happens. It is built, step by step, by the courage of individuals to leave self behind, to love those with whom they are, to persevere in giving of themselves even when their fear of being exploited or unappreciated urges them to put their own interests first. This is an ideal that is really unattainable, one that would break us, if we were to rely on our own strength. The wonderful discovery we make early on in the pilgrimage is that if we can truly even begin to turn from self, a far greater power than our own is opened up for us. In this power we make our commitment; with this power we make our journey.

This reveals to us the vital link between a true Christian community and true personal fidelity to the pilgrimage of prayer. A Christian community is characterized by its quality of being rooted in the experience of transcendence, not otherworldly but truly spiritual. And, as we have said before, the medium of transcendence is silence, the acceptance of the inadequacy of words to bring us into the light of reality. A community that knows the mystery of being silent together, where all hold their hearts in readiness and attentiveness, becomes an embodiment of the light that fills all hearts, the light that is the one Reality all share. This is a church.

The pilgrimage is not a part-time activity—it is the only activity that gives the light of reality to any of our actions. The perseverance and faithfulness that make the pilgrimage fully personal also makes the community of the faithful. The faith of the community results from the faith that springs from the discovery of the light in our hearts. Once we discover this light of Christ and begin to communicate it (because its dynamic is self-giving), then we begin to create the life of Christ in our midst. His life is his presence. And we know his presence through his Body, the community of those who are committed to his enduring light in their hearts, his presence in their lives.

A Benedictine Community in the understanding of St. Benedict's Rule is simply a gathering together of those who journey together with the light of Christ as their guide. It knows this light as love and by their own love for one another they let the light of their guide burn more brightly. It knows the light as an emanation of their Master's Word constantly uttered in their midst and to which they respond with ever deeper attentiveness. The wonder of such a community is that it shares in its Master's victory over all that limits the free passage of his Light. And it is because these limits are passed that a community rooted in the pilgrimage can share its journey with others whose outward circumstances of life are different from those of the monastery but who are also seeking the light and seek to be faithful.

The Benedictine Community spirit is one of largesse, growth, and visionary generosity. Benedict speaks to us of the monastic experience leading to largeness of heart, expansion of consciousness. Those who share in the faithfulness of the community he describes as making rapid progress on their pilgrimage within a love whose tenderness defies description. And here Benedict's wisdom manifests itself as the teaching of the Master. What he is saying to us is that this love whose fullness lies beyond words cannot be described because it can only be known, only experienced in itself. It cannot be remembered or anticipated because it is the supreme reality, the God who IS. Before this reality the last words that have meaning are perhaps those we can take as the inspiration for the community in which our Oblates are now part: Be still and know that I am God.

* * *

Christmas is a feast that can open the hearts of all of us to the presence of Christ. It puts before us the great qualities of innocence and hope that we need if we are to awaken to his light, and it fills us with confidence because it tells us that the old age has ended. The new age, indeed the new creation, has begun and our point of departure for finding it everywhere is finding it a reality in our heart.

Our journey is, then, one to our own hearts. Because all of us are invited to enter this temple and receive this newness of life, we have to recognize this time as a moment to put off everything in us that is dead, everything that prevents us from embracing the mystery of our own creation and entering into the fullness of life we receive as pure gift in the Father's eternal act of creation.

The importance of the teaching of the Incarnation is that the mystery of God in his eternal creativity is not only brought closer to us but really united to us. We no longer need to objectify the mystery that has taken up his dwelling in our hearts of flesh. We now know that our awakening to his reality is an imminent possibility for each of us because the awakening is an incarnate encounter. The joyfulness to which this feast should recall us is that this awakening is not the result of our own power. We are no longer isolated in a dependency on our own inadequate resources. It is not our own power or wisdom that leads us but his love that is present as the light of the supreme reality in our hearts. The humility of the child Jesus is our guide and teacher. In his Light we have Light. In his Love we have Love. In his Truth we are made Truthful.

It is a feast full of wonder and full of hope for all of us, whoever or wherever we are. It is a new dawn for all humankind, one that begins with a faint but certain glow whose strengthening light steadily transforms the sky and earth and grows in brilliance until perfect day. Here in Montreal, as we celebrate the Mass of the Aurora of Christ, the Mass of Dawn, we shall remember all of you. May the New Year to which it gives birth be for each of you a year of new hope and of light.

With every blessing and very much love,

John Main, OSB

Letter Eleven (FEBRUARY 1980)

T he Community at St. Augustine's Monastery in Nassau extended the warmest hospitality during my convalescence. From within the framework of our monastic life I was able to regain my strength and prepare this and another book for publication later in the year.

On my return Montreal was a sunny, snowless city. Our search for a larger site had become urgent. We needed one all the more now that our first monastic candidates were applying to join us. The weekly groups and our other forms of sharing our life resumed straightaway and with new life.

February 21, 1980

My Dearest Friends,

In his chapter on the Observance of Lent, St. Benedict describes it as a season of joy. He tells us to prepare for the great feast of Easter, the center and climax of the Christian year, with the "joy of the Holy Spirit." And, as everywhere else in the Rule, he sees the basis of the Christian response to life's gift as purity of heart, rootedness in prayer.

As we read this chapter of the Rule at Compline last night, at the beginning of Lent in the year we celebrate the 1500th anniversary of St. Benedict's birth, it struck me how unnecessary it is to think of any part of our life in a somber or depressed way. Lent, no less than Christmas or Easter, is full of the Risen Life.

The hardest parts of our life experience point us into freedom. Those are times, of which Lent is a great symbol, when we live through the preparatory stage of the Paschal mystery. And we all need to be prepared for the gift of life, to be ready for it as infinite gift. Lent is a time for preparation like this, when we get ready to enter once again and more deeply into the great awakening of Jesus, his Resurrection. Our preparation itself is joyful because this awakening has already taken place, in time and into eternity. In Jesus the cycle of death and rebirth is definitively completed and perfected because he has broken the cycle that kept man within the finite circle: Jesus has transcended the limitations of human experience that we confront in ourselves during Lent—he has led man into the infinite circle of God, whose "center is everywhere and whose circumference is nowhere." And this is the realm of liberty and joy we enter daily in our prayer.

It is, then, because we observe Lent in the dawn light of Easter that it is a time of joy. The Paschal mystery is completed and we enter into it through the Spirit, preparing ourselves with the silence and stillness of our meditation. There is nothing punitive about Lent. We are not punishing ourselves or being punished. Christians are free of such old religious compulsions because they are free—freed by the forgiveness that gives them fullness of life and that affirms life. Christians enter into the Person who frees them and so, in their turn, Christians forgive those who bear hostility toward them. Perhaps the gift our violent and fear-filled world needs most is forgiveness. And during Lent we deepen our experience of ourselves forgiven and set free of fear—an experience that through the Risen Life we are summoned to communicate to all.

Since writing to you last, I have given talks to Benedictines in St. Louis and Cleveland. My aim in those talks was to share the conviction that monasticism today enjoys a great opportunity. In an age so dissatisfied with its own shallowness—a dissatisfaction that produces so much confusion and violence—the witness of a monastery is to the depth and absolute value of a life centered in Christ. Not merely by ideas, but in the incarnation of their faith in his life, the monk's message to the world is that everything falls apart into chaos when the center is lost; and his message is that Christ is the universal center, the center of each person and of the world.

When we read the sixteenth Chapter of St. John or St. Paul's letter to the Ephesians we can find ourselves filled with the power of this vision of the universal and personal centrality of Christ. But it has always seemed to me that the great difficulty for each of us is to believe that this vision is really possible for us—to make it our vision, not someone else's that we admire as outsiders. It is here that the monastic life seems to me so important. In the monk we should see a man to whom this vision has spoken with absolute value and evoked an absolute personal response. But in the monk we also see an ordinary, weak man. His ordinariness is an essential part of his message. In his ordinary life we see man redeemed from shallowness and inserted deeply into the great order, the essential structure of the universe. We see his life witnessing to the fact that God alone is to be worshipped because he alone is good and his goodness endures eternally. In more contemporary language, his life shows the possibility of founding our life on the reality of absolute value, no longer condemned to the shifting sands of passing fashion.

To try to illustrate the challenge to us as men and women of the twentieth century, I tried to put before the communities in St. Louis and Cleveland an understanding of the Christian life as a call to transcendence. Here again, the monastic life has an essential witness to make.

For St. Benedict, the monastic life was a continuous conversion, not a once-for-all change of status. The ground on which this conversion is realized is the heart of the monk, his most simple and most absolute level of being. And so, his conversion should lead him into an ever deeper authenticity; more and more he should not merely believe what he says but be what he believes. The essential conversion is not concerned with externals because it is not a change from one form to another but from form to essence. The monk's conversion of heart is a conversion of idea into reality. When he encounters the vision of St. John or St. Paul or his own monastic tradition, he opens himself to the personal reality of what they communicate. And, in his openness, that is to say in his prayer, this vision is realized, made real, converted from theory into a living truth.

The dynamic of this conversion is transcendence. And because a total transcendence is involved, a "loss of self," we have to understand transcendence as an expansion of our whole being — a pushing back of the frontiers of our own limitations. It is a dynamic motion, a recentering beyond ourselves and a shedding of all the limitations of self-centeredness, of egoism. And so, the principle of transcendence is a creative development of our whole person, not merely a specialized part of it, not mere imitation, but a deepening of the integral harmony of mind and heart that can only be realized when we are turned away from ourselves. It is the movement of prayer. And in it we begin to find ourselves as persons created for an eternal destiny, one that our self-conscious frame of reference simply cannot comprehend or contain. We find our own true significance no longer in terms of our limitations but of our potentiality for expansion, indeed infinite expansion, in Christ. The monk in his ordinariness is one who is uncovering the sublimity of this essential, human meaning.

Conversion leads through transcendence to union. But how can we say that we find our true meaning if we are truly in union, which means truly absorbed in God? Our modern consciousness holds back from union, and so from transcendence, precisely because it demands always to know what is happening to it — and it fears to take the risk of a union that seems to spell the death of self-awareness. The truth involved here is a paradox and the only way through a paradox is to enter it in person. Paradoxes do not have answers and this is the integral Christian paradox, that the one who wants to find his or her life must first lose it. I think a phrase of Teilard de Chardin's illuminates the paradox for us when he says that "union differentiates." The more we are absorbed into another, the more we become the person we are called to be. And this is the nature of our union with God in Christ. There is indeed no other way to find our selves, our life. Just as we can only know God by the power of his own knowing, so we can ony know ourselves by that same power — for God is the ground of our being. It is the supreme joy and the destiny each one of us is called to, to discover that this power is the power of love. Our origin is in love and our culmination is in love because only love knows.

It is this vision that authenticates the Benedictine's place in the Church and value for the world; and we hope that this year of interiority will deepen our understanding of both of these. A monastery exists precisely to provide the incarnate and participatory context within which the love of Christ can be fully known. St. Benedict's vision in writing the Rule was not to provide monastic "ideals" but to lay down the practical guidelines the living of which would bring men into the experience of the reality of God.

Ideals are so dangerous for all of us. There are so many who want to talk about prayer or read books on prayer or attend courses on prayer. But St. Benedict advised to say as little about prayer as possible—the monk who wants to pray has simply to enter into prayer. Because of this, monasteries have so much to offer the world as places where the turning to Christ, the conversion to Christ, is the clear basis of everything that is done in them. It is not that the monks are supermen but that they have organized their lives with an utterly clear priority. In their conversion they turn from themselves to their brethren in the community, to Christ in prayer, and to God in Christ. This is the clear Benedictine tradition and when it is fully alive in the hearts of men and women, it has the power to convert, to turn to Christ, all who come under its influence.

The love we experience in our monastic life is not in the first place our love for God, but his love for us. And this is the source of our monastic peace, the great treasure we have to share with the world. The harmony of a monastery flows from this knowledge that our beginning and our end, our point of departure and our destination, are both found in the same center, the only center, who is Christ. Now, monks as men of prayer know this not as sublime theory but as practical knowledge given to them by the gift of God's light.

I feel a great sense of urgency to share this with all of you. And it is a wonder and happiness to me that you all take the time and trouble to read these letters and to pass them on to your friends. What I want to say to each of you is to be open to this prayer of Christ yourselves—again, in the most practical way. Meditate every morning and every evening. And in the time of your meditation be poor, be simple: recite your word and only your word.

The marvel of prayer is this: it is transcendence realized. We pass over from self and so the love of Christ is set free in our hearts. All the illusions and images that restrict or distort our vision are transcended. Prayer is the work of finding and realizing our own fully human liberty of spirit—our freedom from desire (even the desire for God), our freedom from sin and from illusion. Desire, sin, and illusion are all transcended because in prayer we are made real by being in harmonious contact with the ground of our being: God's own free-flowing and all-embracing love.

What the monk discovers as, in all humility, he tries to lead his conversion of life is that prayer is not the isolated moment of ecstasy. It is the movement of his whole being from self to God. This movement is the structure of his life and after a lifetime in the monastery it is the structure of his being. His witness is not to an ideal but to a present reality—the reality of the transcendent Presence that summons him to an infinite expansion of spirit.

Thank you again for all your messages of goodwill. I am glad to tell you that after my week of talks and lectures I feel very well. Perhaps my illness has given me a sharpened awareness that life is for living—that we must live fully in the *now*, the moment that is eternal only if we enter it fully.

With much love,

John Main, OSB

Letter Twelve (MAY 1980)

S hortly after our last letter I travelled with Brother Laurence to Victoria, British Columbia at the invitation of the Bishop and the cathedral clergy there. We spent a week, talking twice a day in the Cathedral and to many other groups about meditation. A flourishing group already existed there thanks to a priest who had been a member of the group in Montreal. The people with whom we meditated every morning and evening in the cathedral formed a good cross section of the local society, and many coming to it for the first time told us how the tradition we were sharing with them came as the answer to a long search. Never before had we seen so clearly both how greatly this way is needed and how available it is to the people who understand that the commitment it entails is just what they have been seeking.

After Easter I spent some days at a midweek retreat for priests organized by the core members of our Tuesday morning priests' group. I think we were all amazed at the depth of feeling among us that, in the end, our priesthood and apostolate had to be built on a real, personal commitment to prayer. We talked at length and very openly about what this meant for the Church, but it was above all in the silence of our meditation, three times each day, that our real unity was understood.

Further afield, we visited a group that meets regularly in Plattsburgh, New York, and Dom Laurence visited Toronto to arrange the formation of two groups there which now meet each week, one an ecumenical group meeting at an Anglican religious House, another run by two of our Oblates downtown. On his return he stayed with Bishop Hill in Kingston and spoke to and meditated with a group of young Anglican clergy and their wives.

Our Oblate Community had its first meeting here in March. Most of those who had joined since December were able to attend and to welcome a group of new members. From our more farflung Oblates, in Vancouver and Louisiana we heard how supportive their membership of our spiritual community was to them and how it encouraged their own commitment to prayer as the grounding reality of each day.

May 1, 1980

My Dearest Friends,

When we last wrote it was to say that the deepest Christian understanding of Lent makes it a time of joy. And now, in the middle of the Easter session, we can all understand why. The great ceremonies of Holy Week mirror the stirring of life and beauty in the world around us and remind us that our Lord, who has risen, has awakened to all that is, to the All. And it is because he summons all now to awaken to him that we send you this letter with great joy.

Every year the Easter celebration reveals a little more clearly the depth to which the love of Jesus, his own fullness of life, has penetrated our human hearts. The Easter Vigil repeats the same ceremonies each year but we are never the same people who celebrate them. Each year we have grown in our capacity to understand and enter the mystery of Life they point us toward. We have been made more capable of receiving the revelation of his love—both through our deepening commitment to meditation and through all the many new challenges of our life. And so each year we take another step into full consciousness— toward the full knowledge of the personal mystery that underpins everything we are and do and without which we would lack meaning and purpose. Each year the radical change that the death and resurrection of Jesus has worked in our ability to see God rises a little further in our experience. The risen life that wells up in our heart at prayer and whose tidal flow is felt in every part of our life takes us more confidently into the mystery of Oneness—the mystery that is the Resurrection.

This has been our third Easter in the monastery in Montreal, and I have to feel a sense of wonder at the growth we have been blessed with. We look forward to our first candidates for the novitiate later this year and on June 8 Dom Laurence will be ordained to the priesthood. We have seen our work reach out in many unpredictable ways both in North America and Africa and our own commitment has been encouraged by the serious way many individuals and communities have responded to the pilgrimage of meditation.

The journey is a simple one. It requires a certain vision of its importance, a certain humility to begin, and a certain fidelity and courage to persevere—the willingness, above all, to be led into fullness. These are all essentially human qualities, the qualities needed for any fruitful contact with life, and the journey is an ordinary one. We don't follow it to sensationalize life but to see life—every aspect of it as well as its inner harmony and direction—as the mystery it is. The greatest danger and temptation is to complicate. As far as I can see, if we are actually on the journey—if the poverty of the mantra is the rich core of our lives—then we grow more and more simple. Increasingly, we see the utter simplicity of the call Jesus addresses uniquely to each one of us, to leave all things and self behind and to follow him into the infinite freedom of his union with the Father.

With this as the center of our vision of life all the rest gradually falls into place in the pattern that we are called to bring into ever more resonant harmony. That harmony we may discover in different ways and each moment of discovery is, in a real sense, an eternal moment in which we open our eyes to the divinizing light of Christ. Our life is a growth in simplicity because all things are not bathed in the light and held together, in the new creation of the Resurrection, by it. To see this is to see ourselves also as an integral part of the vital harmony that is Christ. And all that is needed is to look away from ourselves.

This sounds so wonderful we can hardly believe it is real or, if it is real, then possible for us. And yet it only requires that we are on the journey, that we have had the humility to begin and the openness to the power of Christ to persevere, for us to know that this is not only real and possible but essential for us. The complications seem to arise on the side roads and dead ends, not on the straight way we are called to follow. Any of us can wander off on these diversions, into distractions, triviality, self-importance. The great power of liberty and confidence that permeates our life, however, is that we do have a way back to the straight way, to simplicity and othercenteredness. Our way back is simply the love of Jesus that is always present to us, in our own heart, not as something we have either to earn or conjure up—but as something that simply is and is so simply that it underpins and surrounds us in the roots of our being. It loves us into being and cannot leave us until we have freely accepted the gift of being it bestows.

We live in an age that has lost the experience of simplicity and so is losing the experience of growth. We are trained to recognize value only in the illusion of complexity and so we look for the instant. This would be bearable, although miserable, if we could make ourselves in the image of the machines we create. But we cannot. Our humanity demands that we travel to a deeper level of awareness where we see and experience the reality of God, and our hearts are restless until we have learned to be still and silent at this level. There are many spiritual "techniques" that operate at the superficial level of our being where we are carried along on a stream of distraction and that promise "instant" results. No one could confidently say that in the ways of providence people might not be led from these to a more serious and mature commitment. "Sin is behovely," as Dame Julian said. But we need to remind ourselves nonetheless that the stream of distraction is not the ocean of God. It is only too easy to anesthetize ourselves. to be so soaked in our own images or self-reflection that we just drift along, hovering or floating in a realm of self-conscious piety. But it is also possible to take the journey to reality, to be led by Christ the Enlightened One into the great awakening to his Father and to realize our vocation to sanctity. By ourselves we could not make the journey. But we are not by ourselves because we are "in the Spirit." Nor can this experience even be understood just as our own experience. Our vision is the vision of Jesus and our knowledge of God is a oneness with his knowledge.

The call to the deeper level of our being where this union is found cannot be silenced ultimately by any amount of distraction or evasion. It is the Word spoken eternally by the Father and our own being derives from its utterance. If we could finally shut it out we would ourselves immediately cease to be. Listening to the Word and awakening in the full consciousness of God to the point of our creation is the task and raison d'être of our lives. It is the way of our meditation. The challenge of our life and the deep responsibility of the Church as the community of those who are faithful to the pilgrimage is to show that this is the way for all people. To show that we can become simple only if we turn from self-centeredness, from trying to find our center in ourselves. Because our center is in God we have to turn beyond ourselves to him.

Our growth into this experience of God, of the liberty of spirit that comes from othercenteredness, is entirely natural. We have simply to clear the ground and to be open to the energy of God's love that makes it possible for us to enter his mystery of communion. The task is to be simple and open and to remain open while the process of growth unfolds itself in our heart and throughout our lives. Like every process of growth, the condition for it is patience. We are usually trained to distrust patience as a waste of time: and in a world-view tied to the finite dimension, time seems the most precious of all values. In a real sense it is precious because it is through time and in time that we are each called to awaken to the eternal. But what we have to recover is the knowledge that the right use of time is patience. Time is given to teach us patience, to teach us to be still.

Any technique of prayer is by definition impatient. It sets out to make things happen according to the desire we have for God, to possess God—a desire that operates within the limitations of our sense of time. It will, then, be a disposable method, used until it produces a desired effect, then dropped and taken up again when we want more.

When we were in Victoria, a college student who had come to the cathedral "to find out what 'Christian meditation' was about" attended the nightly meeting of the meditation group. In the discussion period after meditation he asked a question. He began by saying that he was familiar with many techniques of prayer, mainly from the East, but was not very familiar with the Christian tradition. Why, he asked, did we seem to be making such an absolute claim for the Christian tradition of meditation? Was the Benedictine tradition derived from John Cassian really so different from the others? I think we have to understand why this question could be asked to understand in what type of world the Gospels have to be preached today. And I think we have to be sure from our own experience of the answer that a Christ-centered life provides if we are to be able to communicate the Gospels as a living tradition.

We suggested to him what I have just said about the nature of techniques—a technique is a goal-oriented thing, necessary if we are involved in learning how to drive a car or grow roses but disastrous if we are learning the way of unlearning, the way of prayer. A technique, in the realm of spirit, intensifies our self-centeredness. But why, then, is meditation in the Christian tradition so much more than a technique? First, because it is to be understood as a discipline, a way we follow regardless of our immediate experience, a way that takes us steadily beyond immature slavery to our passing moods and desires into the liberty of the children of God. It is a discipline in the richest and most positive sense of the word: a learning, a discipleship, a yoke (meaning "union") that Jesus tells us is necessary but light. Any way of life is, I suppose, in a sense either a technique or a discipline. Techniques are limited to a restricted area of experience, whereas the creative discipline grows to include and harmonize the whole of our lives.

Contrary to a prevalent belief, commitment sets us free, seriousness brings us joy, and discipline leads us to transcendence. This is the context in which we are called to communicate the Gospels and our Christian tradition of prayer. To underestimate the absolute demand the Gospels present to each of us is to underestimate the absolute joy and fullness of life it offers. We have to be clear in our own minds, then, that we are communicating not a short excusion but a way that spans our lives, a way that St. Paul tells us "begins in faith and ends in faith."

The answer to the young man in Victoria is really "faith"—that is the difference. Meditation in the Christian way is the way of faith. Christ is our way to the Father. Christ is our faith. His power supports us in the journey that we are summoned to undertake in the freedom in which we were created and by which God can call us to share, as St. Peter tells us, in his own nature.

When we begin to meditate it is natural to wonder, "How long will this take?" We need to be told—and our living tradition tells us—that it takes no time at all. This is the same as saying that it takes only as long as it takes us to realize that it takes no time. This is why the real use of time is patience. In the moment of pure patience, simple openness, the little ego that keeps us self-centered fades away in the nothing it came from and our spirit, centered in Christ, flows into the plenitude of God as its beginning and its end, its alpha and omega. Our faith is our patience, our openness to what already is, because we are not waiting so much for God to arrive as for ourselves to realize he is with us in Christ, Emmanuel, God-with-us. What we have to learn is not to "make God happen" but to become sufficiently still, sufficiently silent, to allow the consciousness of Jesus, his Spirit within us, to expand and push back the frontiers of our limitations, to reveal to us that we are in God.

To pray deeply is to be faithful. To be filled with faith is no less than to be filled with the power of the love of Jesus—which is the selfsame love with which he is loved by the Father. His openness to the Father opens our heart to the Spirit. Our greatest challenge is our greatest opportunity: to become faith-filled, to root and found ourselves in Christ as the source and being of our faith.

This is just what we do as we follow the way of meditation. Every day is built into the faith with which we leave self behind and journey into the mystery of God: the faith we open ourselves to each morning and each evening. And our mantra is the way of faith and the sacrament of love. To say our word continuously throughout the time of our meditation is our simple task. What could be simpler? But as we know, simplicity is not simplistic: commitment makes compromise a false option. The way to simplicity must be itself simple; we have great cause to rejoice that in the mantra we have found this way.

The way of the mantra is a way of generosity, of expansion and deepening, not in any sense a way of exclusion or narrowmindedness. It is a mystery of this journey that it makes us grow in our sensitivity to the presence of God and the goodness of his working in many unexpected areas of our lives. It is not always easy to explain how this is so, and indeed it cannot really be known outside of the experience. To turn from our thoughts and imagination at the time of prayer and to be wholly faithful to our simple task of saying the "one little word"—how can you explain by image or concept that this way is into the silence in which God reveals himself in Jesus as the source and foundation of all creation? Yet we know, when we have followed this way even for a little while, that the poverty of the mantra enriches us in a movement of love that fills every part of our life and awakens us to the mystery in which we are inserted—the mystery that is closed to us as long as we remain centered in ourselves rather than in him.

We have to understand what it means to be simple and to discover, from our own experience, the dynamic truth that we become simple by becoming othercentered. Although we are all trained to put our trust in complexity, I think we know at a deep level of our being that real, inner peace depends upon our going beyond complexity and becoming simple. The wonder of the Christian revelation is that while outside of Christ all is centerless and complex, we find our simplicity by discovering ourselves in union with him—and he himself is our peace. In and through our meditation we come to know that this peace is not a passive stillness, not any kind of negation. It is pure affirmation, as is the faith and poverty of our mantra. Also, it reveals itself progressively as nearness, our nearness to the source of all creation. We know, as St. Paul tells us, that in Christ we, who were once far off, have been brought near, and world which was without hope has now been filled, made radiant with the knowledge of our nearness to the Father.

The Christian who awakens to this mystery has, by the nature of the experience itself, the experience of love, to communicate it. There are many, shaped by our materialistic values today, who would say that this Christian vision is illusory—a myth of yesterday's world. And there are some who would say that it may be true but only for the few. No one can, of course, quantify God's revelation and gift of himself. This is the deepest and most personal movement of his love and it is absolute. But if our faith is in harmony with that of the New Testament, we can only believe that the words Jesus spoke were addressed to all men, and the letters St. Paul wrote, containing the highest claims ever made about man's involvement with God, were written to the ordinary men and women of the first Christian communities. The call is universal. Our greatest fault as Christians has been that we have come so tragically to underestimate both the universality and the wonder of our revelation. There is nothing worse than a shallow Christianity. We are not invited to hover in the netherworld of our own ideas and images but are summoned to go beyond all our limitations, all the restrictions of self-consciousness and to expand to infinity in the heart of the Trinity.

We are called to realize that the power and energy of creation flows in our hearts and that this power is the energy of love. Upon it, upon its wellspring in Christ, our peace depends. To find this peace, more is required than knowing ourselves. Our destiny is to know that we are known—that our roots are in God. In our meditation we discover the resonant harmony between the being of God and our being. As we all know, language fails us, but we have to try to use it to direct our attention to the mystery and its depths. There the mantra leads us and, like God's harmonic, it roots itself in our heart until every part of our heart is opened to his love and his power can pour freely into us.

Sainthood and wisdom are simply names for reality. God alone is real. And what we discover in meditation and our daily fidelity is that the godliness we are summoned to is full sanity, flowing from the full power of God's love. Each of us, by the very fact that we have been given being, that we have begun to share in the reality of God himself, is invited to discover that goodness and godliness flow freely in the depths of our heart.

The wonder of the Christian revelation is that this is not theological poetry but that each of us does have infinite importance. Our creation is designed in a mysterious way by God to fulfill the design of his own perfection. When we have turned to him we reflect back to him the glory he has given us. This is our meaning, our vocation. And it is in Christ that we turn. We could neither know nor realize our destiny without Jesus who awoke to it in his human consciousness and who has realized it in the Spirit he sends into our heart. "In Christ the complete being of the Godhead dwells embodied and in him you have been brought to completion."

Each Easter the experience of Jesus revealed to us calls

forth a deeper response from us and we grow a little further into the completion he brings us. To commit ourselves to this growth is the greatest opportunity any of us could ever have. In the brotherhood we share in him, let me urge you to deepen your own commitment to the simplicity that we need for this growth. We keep you all in our hearts on this pilgrimage.

Wishing you every blessing,

John Main, OSB